Coast Salish
THEIR ART AND CULTURE

REG ASHWELL

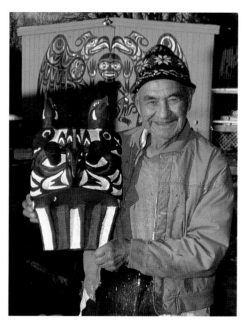

Dedicated to Chief Simon Charlie for his lifelong commitment to art, culture and humanitarianism.

hancock
house

For Thousands of Years

For thousands of years
I have spoken the language of the land
and listened to its many voices.
I took what I needed
and found there was plenty for everyone.
The rivers were clear and thick with life,
the air was pure and gave way
to the thrashing of countless wings.
On land, a profusion of creatures abounded.
I walked tall and proud
knowing the resourcefulness of my people,
feeling the blessings of the Supreme Spirit.
I lived in the brotherhood of all beings.
I measured the day
by the sun's journey across the sky.
The passing of the year was told
by the return of the salmon
or the birds pairing off to nest.
Between the first campfire and the last
of each day I searched for food,
made shelter, clothing and weapons,
and always found time for prayer.

— Chief Dan George
from *The Best of Chief Dan George*

Coast Salish

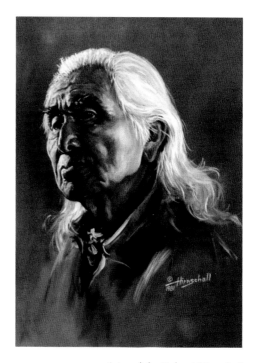

Artwork by Helmut Hirnschall

ISBN 0-88839-620-1
EAN 9780888396204
Copyright © 2006 David Hancock

Cataloging in Publication Data

Ashwell, Reg, 1921 –
    Coast Salish : their art, culture and legends / Reg Ashwell.
ISBN 0-88839-620-1
    1. Coast Salish Indians—History. 2. Coast Salish art. I. Title.

E99.S21A88 2006   971.1004'9794   C2005-906695-4

Printed in Indonesia—TK PRINTING

Editor: Theresa Laviolette
Photo reseacher/writer: Venetia Inglis
Image editor: Laura Michaels
Production: Mia Hancock
Cover design: Rick Groenheyde, Mia Hancock
Photography: David Hancock unless otherwise credited.

Title page image: **Transition I** *(1988) — Marvin Oliver*

Published simultaneously in Canada and the United States by

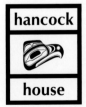

HANCOCK HOUSE PUBLISHERS LTD.
19313 Zero Avenue, Surrey, B.C. Canada V3S 9R9
(604) 538-1114 Fax (604) 538-2262

HANCOCK HOUSE PUBLISHERS
1431 Harrison Avenue, Blaine, WA U.S.A. 98230-5005
(604) 538-1114 Fax (604) 538-2262

Website: **www.hancockhouse.com**
Email: **sales@hancockhouse.com**

Contents

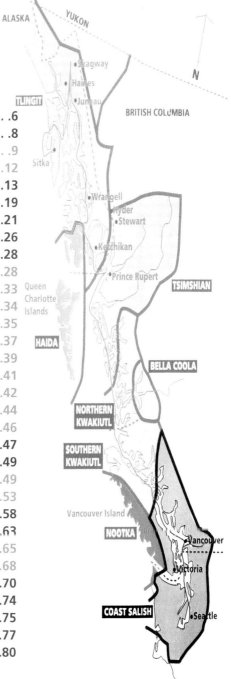

FOREWORD

"Yonder sky, that has wept tears of compassion upon our fathers for centuries untold, and which to us looks eternal, may change. Today is fair; tomorrow it may be overcast with clouds. My words are like the stars that never change.

"There was a time when our people covered the whole land as the waves of a wind-ruffled sea cover its shell-paved floor, but that time has long since passed away, with the greatness of tribes that are now but a mournful memory.

"Every part of this country is sacred to my people. Every hillside, every valley, every plain and grove, has been hallowed by some fond memory or some sad experience of my tribe.

"Even the rocks, which seem to lie dumb as they swelter in the sun along the silent sea shore in solemn grandeur, thrill with memories of past events connected with the lives of my people.

"The noble braves, fond mothers, glad, happy-hearted maidens, and even the little children, who lived and rejoiced here for a brief season, and whose very names are now forgotten, still love these somber solitudes and their deep fastnesses which, at even-tide, grow shadowy with the presence of dusky spirits.

"Our dead never forget this beautiful world that gave them being. They still love its winding rivers, its great mountains and its sequestered vales, and they ever yearn in tender fond affection over the lonely-hearted living, and often return to visit, guide, and comfort them."

— Excerpts from the famous speech delivered in 1854 by Chief Seattle, the great Suquamish Indian leader.

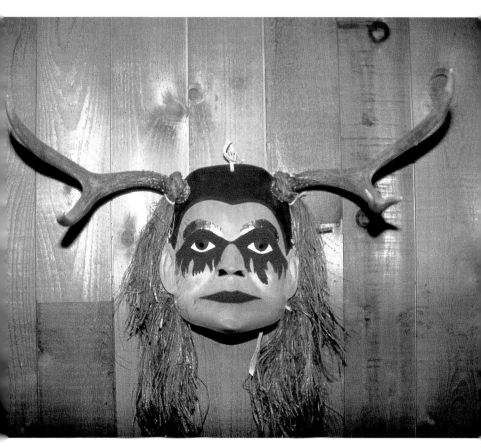

Deer mask. Xa:ytem Native Heritage Centre.

COAST SALISH

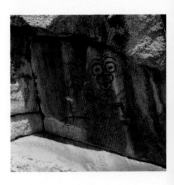

Salish cave drawings at Pitt Lake. The petroglyph features the Slumack or Shumack legend.

The Coast Salish people are unique among the Indians of the Pacific Northwest. They acquired much of northern Native culture, yet they have strong historic connections with the Indians of the Interior. Widely dispersed throughout the coastal areas of southern British Columbia and Washington State, and with footholds far inland along the lower reaches of the Fraser River, the Coast Salish occupied a diversified environment and thus acquired a variety of cultural traits.

The most numerous of the Northwest Coast tribes, in British Columbia alone the Coast Salish numbered 12,000, according to population census of 1835. By 1915 the usual plagues and diseases brought about by the coming of Europeans had reduced the population to only 4,120, their lowest numbers.

The Coast Salish inhabited the coast of the mainland from Bute Inlet in British Columbia to the Columbia River, dividing Washington and Oregon and those areas on Vancouver Island not occupied by the Kwakiutl and the Nootka Indians, from Johnstone Straight to Port San Juan. They also occupied vast areas of western Washington State.

(below) Coast Salish summer shelter.

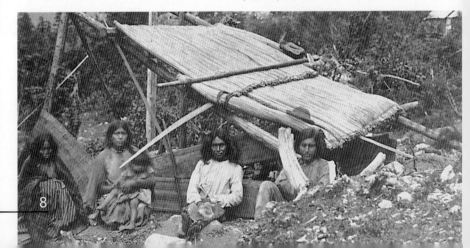

Origins

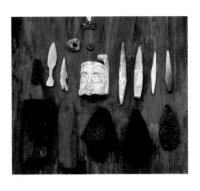

Artifacts such as spearheads or choppers provide windows into the lives of the people who occupied these lands in the distant past.

There is evidence to suggest that the Coast Salish originally migrated to the Northwest Coast in successive waves, coming from the Interior Plateau on the upper reaches of the Fraser and Thompson Rivers. There are definite language characteristics linking the Coast Salish with their Interior Salish brothers. There are also striking similarities between the artifacts found in coast shell mounds and those discovered in some of the ancient burial grounds of the more easterly Interior Salish groups.

The early writings of Charles Hill-Tout, who had close contact with the Salish people in early times, also suggest a strong cultural link between the Coast and Interior Salish people.

Such evidence is strengthened by the several obvious differences that existed between the Coast Salish and other Northwest Coast tribes. Differences in the style of essential tools — such as axes, hammers, and the like — in the construction of their long houses, and in the Coast Salish art forms, which were noticeably much less developed, lead us to the conclusion that the Coast Salish originated from separate cultural backgrounds to those of the other Northwest Coast linguistic groups.

From the pre-historic evidence found in the many shell mounds existing throughout the coastal area, it may be assumed with reasonable accuracy that the Salish migration to the Pacific coast took place only a few centuries before the coming of the European Explorers.

We can only speculate on what might have caused such a migration over a difficult and dangerous terrain. It may have been a result of one of the endless wars that took place among the many bands that comprised the Interior Salish, or a sudden scarcity of game, or population pressures, or perhaps the haphazardly nomadic wanderings of a few hardy souls.

Whatever the reasons, we can assume that the Salish migration took place in a series of nomadic groups and not as a warlike nation bent on conquering new territory.

And so they came, bypassing the unnavigable waters of the Fraser Canyon, in the vicinity of Lytton and Hope, by crossing the great rugged Coast Range Mountains and journeying into a new and beautiful land of gentler climate, teeming with the food resources of the Fraser River Delta and the coastal waterways.

Did the newcomers migrate to a vast, unoccupied territory? Or did they find a small pre-Salish population, maintaining its own language and culture, yet too few in numbers — or perhaps simply disinclined — to resist the invaders? There are indications that such a population did indeed exist but were eventually absorbed by the Salish, who continued to arrive in ever-increasing numbers as word of this new land of plenty spread back to relatives and friends left behind.

If there was a fusion and blending of cultures between the Salish and an older civilization, it may account for the rather noticeable differences in the physical appearance between the Coast Salish and their ancestors from the Interior.

Coast Salish people were usually shorter in stature and less slender than the Interior Indians. Their hair varied from black to dark reddish brown. Dark eyes carried little of the slightly Asian slant that so often characterized the Interior and Plains Indians.

From Spuzzum on the lower Fraser River, the Salish gradually paddled via navigable waters into the mainland territory around the mouth of the river. Following the sea-lanes northward, they eventually reached as far as Bute Inlet. Finally they occupied the San Juan and Gulf Islands and parts of Vancouver Island, penetrating as far north as the Salmon River.

As they traveled westward via the waterways to the Pacific coast, the newcomers must indeed have thought that they had reached a land of milk and honey — a veritable *temlaham*, or paradise — the Gitksan Garden of Eden of which Barbeau wrote so dramatically in his *Downfall of Temlaham*; a land very different from the country they had left behind with its hot, short summers, followed by long, bitterly cold winters.

10

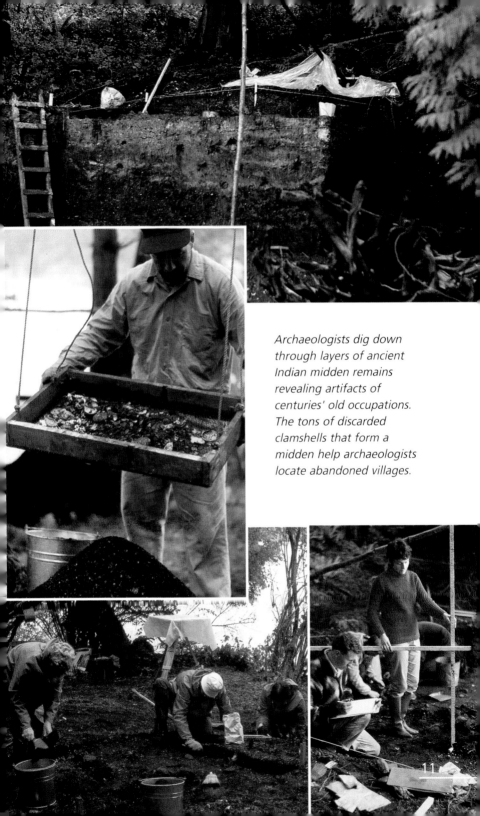

Archaeologists dig down through layers of ancient Indian midden remains revealing artifacts of centuries' old occupations. The tons of discarded clamshells that form a midden help archaeologists locate abandoned villages.

11

The Land

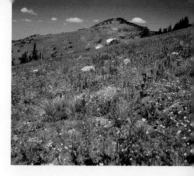

Manning Park meadow filled with wild flowers. Many types of flowers and berries were collected to make the dyes used to color Salish blankets.

The Coast Salish found a new land of dense forests with a heavy growth of fir, cedar, spruce, hemlock, and pine. Due to the prevailing moist climate, the evergreens reach awesome heights, and the heavy undergrowth causes much of the great-forested areas to become all but impenetrable by land.

North to Bute Inlet, the most northerly extent of Coast Salish settlement, the heavily timbered, mountainous terrain of the interior extends to the very edge of a deeply indented shoreline. In the coastal areas the winters are mild with many sunless days of mist and rain. Further inland, in the river valleys, an easier topography prevails. Birch, alder, poplar, maple, and willow trees replace the giant evergreens. Here the climate is more extreme with greater snow accumulation in the uplands.

To the Salish people, migrating from harsher climes, this new land must have appeared to be a paradise of great natural wealth. Wealth to them, of course, had nothing to do with precious metals or stones, such as gold and silver or diamonds and rubies. The wealth lay in the teeming supplies of natural food resources. There were fish in abundance in the rivers and in the open sea; game abounded in the forests; and in the more open areas wild berries grew in profusion, and bulbs and roots could be dug from the rich soil with relative ease.

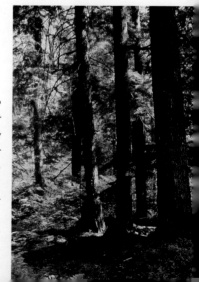

Manning Park forest. Coastal people would travel in small groups into their forested lands, setting up temporary hunting camps during the summer months. Each group would return home with the bales of meat, skins, and many other useful materials that they had collected on their journey, preserved for use in the winter.

HOUSING

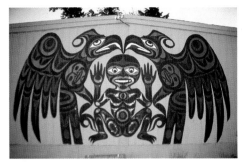

House front painting of two Thunderbirds and a man, Duncan, B.C. Thunderbird is a supernatural being that is revered by all the Northwest Coast cultures. It is thought to be an enormous bird whose flight brings thunderstorms to the coast. Its reptile-like lightening bolts kept in its mountain lair, are sent darting though the sky with a blink of its eyes.

The great stands of tall, straight red cedar trees were eminently suitable for the building of communal style dwellings and the Coast Salish constructed huge, grandly spacious houses, far removed from the almost subterranean, dark, and airless structures built as permanent winter homes in their ancestral homeland among the Interior Salish. The Coast Salish occasionally built *kekuli,* or semi-subterranean houses, in early times and examples of them have been recorded at Point Grey, Howe Sound, and Bute Inlet.

From the red cedar Coast Salish men hollowed out their dugout canoes and carved the masks for their shamanistic rituals and ceremonial dances. In later years, under the cultural influences of the Kwakiutl and other Northwest Coast tribes, the Coast Salish carved inside house-posts for their longhouses. The fur traders and early explorers also noted grave figures.

Also from the prized cedar tree the women stripped the bark, always careful not to injure or kill the tree by taking too much at one time. The precious bark was put to innumerable uses, including weaving short, fringed skirts for everyday wear, and making fine baskets that were used as containers for gathering berries, roots, bulbs, clams, and other necessities of life.

The importance of the western red cedar to the Indian tribes of the Northwest Coast cannot be over emphasized, especially in the pre-European era before the use of iron and steel. Native people used only stone tools for building the longhouses, hollowing out canoes, and making wooden containers such as buckets and storage boxes. It was the relatively soft wood of the cedar that made carpentry with stone tools possible. The wood is so straight-grained it can be split into sections with stone or even elk horn wedges. In older times, before intensive logging, the mighty cedar trees — growing on the coastal strip from Northern California to Southern Alaska — towered as high as two hundred feet. Most of the great trees have been cut down now but you can still see the stumps, sometimes measuring six or more feet across.

Early pioneers arriving in Northwest Coast harbors were amazed at the size of the huge wooden plank houses lining the shores. Made by people who had only stone hammers and wedges of wood or horn, they were incredible structures.

The Coast Salish houses sometimes reached extreme proportions. The great Chief Seattle (Sealthh), after whom the City of Seattle was named, owned a house 100 feet (thirty meters) long that held ten families. His brother built a special feast house 540 feet (160 meters) long. And according to an account by explorer Simon Fraser (for whom the Fraser River was named), he once entered a chief's house that measured 640 feet (190 meters) in length by sixty feet wide (eighteen meters). All of the interior apartments are described as being square except the chief's, which was ninety feet long (twenty-seven meters). The houses were not always this large, and indeed the lodges of the common people would have been considerably smaller.

The Coast Salish houses were usually built in a shed style, with the flat roofs gently pitched because of the great width of the structures, inclining upward from front to rear. The Coast Salish found these roofs very useful for drying fish, and they also used them as handy platforms for viewing the potlatches and other ceremonial gatherings and festivities. Moreover, the sloping roofs were advantageous in shedding rain. By grooving the wide cedar boards of the roof lengthwise in a flat U shape, and then arranging them alter-

Coast Salish eagle, outside house pole. Tsawwassen B.C.

Coast Salish welcoming figure. Xa:ytem Native Heritage Centre

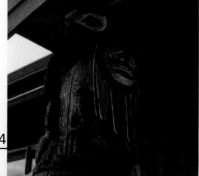
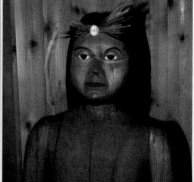

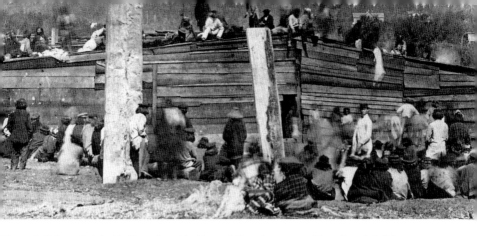

Coast Salish potlatch. Unlike other Northwest Coast communities, Coast Salish potlatches could be sponsored by any respected member of the community. Class lines were not well defined, allowing an industrious commoner to advance himself through marriage connections or accumulation of wealth. (Photo: Royal B.C. Provincial Archives.)

nately so that the flange of one board was turned down to fit into the upturned flange of the next, the rain was diverted into a series of channels and carried to the lower edge of the roof.

A heavy individual framework, independent of the walls, supported the roofs of the longhouses. There were two basic methods employed in putting on the wall planks. They could be placed horizontally, one above the other, and tied to the framework, or to extra upright posts, by cedar withes. But the most usual, and certainly the simplest method, was to place the wall boards upright and hold them vertically by driving their ends deep into the earth.

Cracks in the walls were sometimes chinked with moss and usually they were covered on the inside with mats. But the cracks were useful in that they kept a good circulation of air in the house and allowed the escape of any residue smoke from the lodge fires that had not found its way through the holes in the roof that were left for that purpose.

The floors of the longhouses were usually earth, sometimes dug down but usually left at ground level. Some families sprinkled the earth with sand. Others laid down hand woven mats as carpeting. In the house of a wealthy chief, the floor might be covered with planks.

Dug into the floors were shallow pits for fireplaces and these pits were often walled with stones or heavy timbers to prevent the fires from spreading. The number of fire pits depended on the size of the house. A two-family house was one large room, with a fire pit

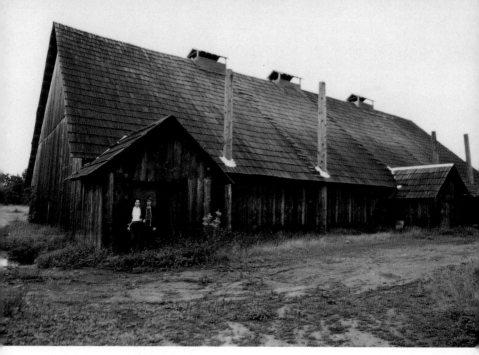

Tzeachten ceremonial house, Sardis, B.C.

Interior of Tzeachten ceremonial house, Sardis B.C. Coast Salish houses were designed to house multiple related families. Each family had its own fireplace and occupied a corner of the house. If there were more than four families, additional fire pits would be placed along the sides of the house, as each family was responsible for their own food stocks and cooking.

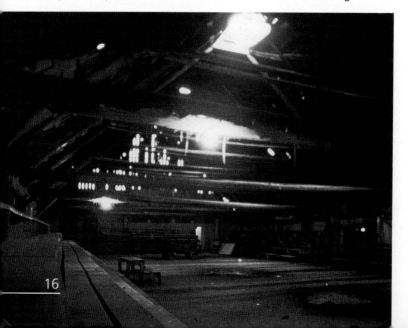

at each end. Four family houses had a fire close to each corner. The really large houses, such as chiefs' houses, were divided up into compartments, each with its own fire. These compartments, occupying the space between two uprights, were usually about ten or twelve feet (three to four meters) wide. The walls were often made by standing vertical planks on the earthen floor, with their tops resting against the crossbeams. Alternately, if the planks were scarce, rush mats could be hung from the cross beams.

Since the Coast Salish knew nothing of glass before the coming of Europeans, their houses had no windows, although the larger houses had several doors. Even the smaller houses had at least two doors, one at the front to be used as an entrance, and an "escape" door most likely placed on a side of the house facing the forest. The doors were covered with a curtain of deer or elk skins. If it was felt that a danger of enemy attack existed, planks were piled up against the openings from inside. In the case of some Coast Salish bands, such as the Quinault, the front or main door was an oval opening, raised about three feet from the ground. The door was just large enough for an adult to squeeze through — a deliberate arrangement planned so that an enemy who was rash enough to attempt an entry found it a slow procedure, and could be quickly overcome by the watchful occupants, armed with clubs and poised to attack.

Indeed, the longhouse was at all times an important fortification against enemy attack, with the stout cedar planks providing protection for the occupants who vigorously directed their arrows through crevices in the walls, often with telling effect.

Coast Salish houses contained little in the way of furniture. Raised sleeping platforms, about four feet (120 centimeters) wide and approximately the same distance from the ground, were built around three walls. In front of them, other platforms were built for use as seats, about two feet (sixty centimeters) high and also useful as a step up to the sleeping quarters.

Large drying racks, supported by the cross beams and used especially for drying salmon, were an ever-present necessity in the longhouses. High shelves were often built around the space under the roof slope where there was always a good circulation of air.

These shelves made excellent storage spaces for dried clams and other food supplies that rotted easily. Holes were also dug in the ground, below the bunk or seats, where additional food could be

stored at a controlled temperature. Storage boxes and baskets were packed tightly on platforms and seats not used for sitting or sleeping, and even placed on extra shelves slung from the cross beams.

The interior of the Coast Salish long house was remarkably tidy and cozy looking. The sleeping platforms, with their bedding of fur robes and bird skins, looked comfortable and inviting. The multi-purpose rush mats were everywhere. They were used as carpets on the floor and as spreads on the bunks. They hung as partitions or over shelves, and often covered some of the wall cracks. Clean ones were always kept handy for a guest to sit on or to be used as tablemats. Items kept on the floor, such as cooking stones and storage boxes, were arranged in as neat and orderly a fashion as possible.

Sometimes the Coast Salish men built a work shed outside the longhouse and retired there to make their adzes and hammers, or perhaps to carve a mask, ladle, or bowl, while the women-folk carried on with their cooking and other chores, such as making new rush mats or weaving the famous Salish blankets.

Not all Coast Salish longhouses were of the shed type, with long gently slopping roofs. The Sechelt band, for example, built their longhouses in the Kwakiutl style using a gabled roof.

During the summer months the Coast Salish all but abandoned their winter longhouses and journeyed away on prolonged camping trips, returning for a week or two, staying just long enough to organize another trip. Food had to be gathered and stored for the winter months ahead. This involved land hunting and fishing for the men and related work for the women, who fitted their work to suit their husbands' activities, using days when they were not needed to attend to the process of meat or fish drying.

While the men fished, the women dug for shellfish and gathered clams; or during inland hunting trips, while the men went after game, the women picked berries or dug for roots and bulbs. Children, of course, accompanied their elders and assisted in the work as an essential part of their training. During these nomadic months, they lived in the open or under temporary makeshift shelters.

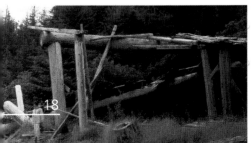

The remains of a longhouse. House boards were valued possessions, if the owners moved they would bring the house boards with them to the new location, leaving the abandoned house frame standing in place.

TRADE

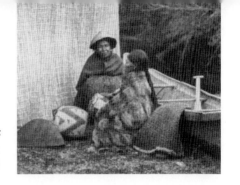

*Temporary summer shelters
were made of mats.*
(Photo: E.S. Curtis Collection)

Like all the Indians of the Pacific Northwest, and indeed throughout
the Americas, the Coast Salish traded with well-established calculat-
ed values in shells (including the coveted abalone shell), coppers,
slaves, hides, ivory, basketry, blankets, and various forms of art
work. Neighboring bands, such as the Songhees of Vancouver Island
and Klallum of Washington, traded extensively with each other.

New trade areas opened up with the horse-mounted Indians of
the dry interior country to the east, and exposed the Northwest Coast
tribes to new ideas. They even traded occasionally for the feathered
war bonnets of the Plains and Kootenay Indians, admiring such finery without much need or use for it, yet taking great delight in the
rows of eagle feathers with their quill-worked headbands.

With the advent of trading posts east of the Rockies and the
arrival of the Russians in Alaska, Northwest Coast tribes gained
access to items displaying beautiful colors which before had been
only visually apparent in the form of sunsets over still waters, or
perhaps the reds and golds of autumn leaves. The Hudson's Bay
Company and Russian traders exchanged colored glass beads and
ornaments dear to the Indian's heart in order to obtain the robes of
animal furs that the Indians wore so casually in cold weather.

Trade intensified with the coming of explorers and traders who
were eager for the fabulously profitable fur pelts. In order to obtain
the goods the traders desired, the Coast Salish and other Northwest
Coast Natives abandoned age-old beliefs that forbade the killing of
wildlife except for the immediate necessities of life, and aided in the
wholesale slaughter of fur-bearing animals. Most sought after were
the soft, glossy pelts of the sea otter and, as a result, these beautiful,
intelligent little mammals were exterminated along the British
Columbia and Washington coasts by the early 1900s despite last
minute efforts to save them.

The rifle replaced the bow and arrow and spear, making it easi-

er and faster to kill animals. Stone tools gave way to iron hammers and steel bladed knives. Wooden receptacles, such as bowls for holding fish oil and ladles made of alder, yew or maple, and of course the incredible storage boxes — which were produced by steaming the soft cedar, bending it into shape, and then lacing the single join with twisted cedar rope — all these passed into obsolescence as the Native people became more dependent on the manufactured hardware and other goods so easily obtainable at the trade store.

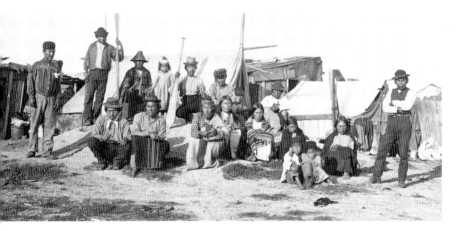

(above) Groups of Coast Salish Indians camped around settlements to facilitate trading. (Photo: Museum of Man and Nature)

(below) Summer encampment at Comox. (Photo: Museum of Man and Nature)

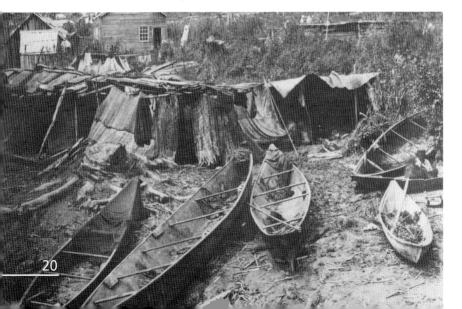

CLOTHING

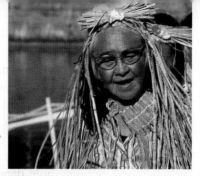

Mary Amos, dressed in traditional West Coast cedar attire.

Traders, aware of the Indians' love of color, brought glass beads and baubles from Venice and the Far East. In those days Venice was renowned as the glass center of the world.

The Indians of the Northwest Coast, not appreciating at first the huge discrepancies in values that favored the greedy traders, eagerly traded their prized fur pelts for glass beads in radiant colors that they had until then only seen in birds' plumage. They augmented or replaced their own beads and shell ornaments of brown and white with beautiful glass beads from far-off lands.

The hexagons in rich blues, brought by the Russians from Venice, were particularly popular and have been found in Indian graves — silent proof of the esteem in which these colorful baubles were held by their owners. Today the old trade beads have a new value; they have become highly collectible and much sought after for their historic significance.

Exciting metals such as brass, silver, and copper were also available from the traders. Coast Salish women historically tied sinews around their ankles for a beautifying effect. They replaced these with shiny copper anklets, sometimes wearing five or six on one ankle.

The Northwest Coast Indians were creative and artistic, innovative, and eager to experiment with new ideas. Soon the more northerly tribes — the Tlingit, Haida, Tsimshian, and Kwakiutl — began designing their own metal ornaments. Silver dollars were beaten down and shaped and engraved to make beautiful bracelets, pendants, and brooches with exciting Northwest Coast designs depicting beaver, bear, killer whale, shark, raven, and eagle, to mention but a few. They were eagerly sought-after up and down the coast, and worn with great pride by the wealthy classes.

Coast Salish women wore a fringed skirt of shredded cedar bark or of rushes fastened at the waist. The men very often wore nothing at all. In rainy weather, capes of cedar bark or rushes were worn,

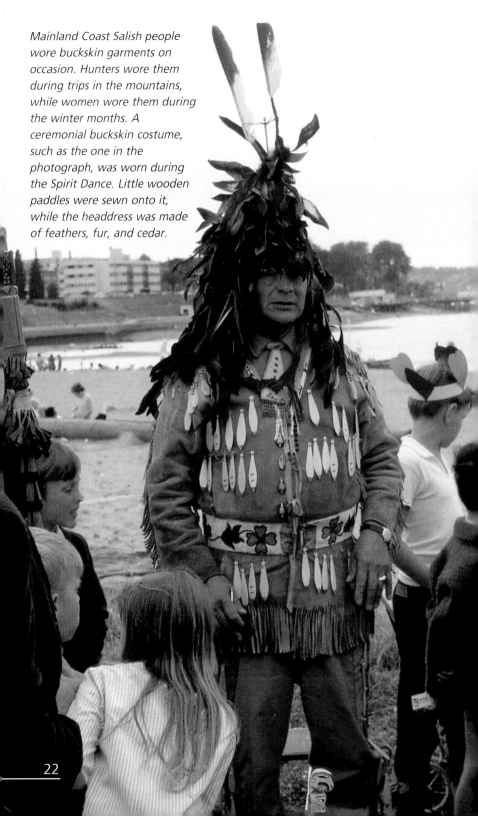

Mainland Coast Salish people wore buckskin garments on occasion. Hunters wore them during trips in the mountains, while women wore them during the winter months. A ceremonial buckskin costume, such as the one in the photograph, was worn during the Spirit Dance. Little wooden paddles were sewn onto it, while the headdress was made of feathers, fur, and cedar.

their smooth woven surfaces being ideal for shedding the water. Inside the houses, the capes were removed so that the wearers did not catch cold in their wet garments.

But woven capes of cattails and cedar bark were not sufficient covering during the long, cold winters, especially for the upriver Salish who lived in a land of easier topography. In that area, trees such as birch, willow, alder, and maple usurped the dense forests of giant evergreens. The wet, foggy, and near sunless days of the long winters of the coastal areas were frequently supplanted by heavy snows and bitter cold.

The Coast Salish fashioned cold weather robes for themselves from almost any skin of bird or beast. According to early accounts, when the Indians, wearing their beautiful mantles of sea otter, martin, and lynx, boarded the ships of the explorers, the foreigners were amazed at the beauty of the many fine pelts and quick to realize the wealth to be attained in trade for the valuable furs.

Coast Salish women prepared the furs by scraping the insides and rubbing them with animal brains kept for the purpose. Large skins, such as bearskins, could be worn whole. Sea otter pelts were smaller and five or six had to be sewn together. This was accomplished by making holes with bone awls, and drawing thin strips of skin through them in rough stitches.

Leggings and moccasins were not popular with the Coast Salish, who usually preferred to go barefoot. The moist climate of the coastal areas was not suitable for buckskin footwear because the wet leather first leaked and then dried out as stiff as a board.

Tribal clothing styles were the last thing to change. But with the opening of a Hudson's Bay Company trading post at Vancouver, near Portland, in 1826 and the subsequent appearance of the famous Hudson's Bay blankets, the old styles gave way to different modes of dress.

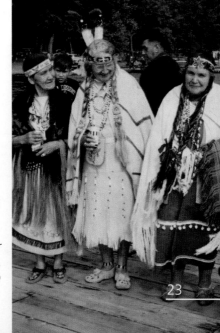

Plateau-style clothing is often worn for festive occasions. Cultus Lake, B.C.
(Photo: W. Jilek)

23

The fur traders of those early days got along well with their Indian brothers and did not consciously attempt to interfere with Native lifestyles. But changes resulting from such contact were inevitable. Furs the Salish once used for cloaks went into the Hudson's Bay storehouses and the Salish replaced them with store-bought woolen blankets, most of them a drab gray in color.

Yet it was not until after settlers began to arrive in numbers and missionaries were sent in among the Natives that drastic changes came about.

The Coast Salish were among the first of the Northwest Coast Indians to be seriously affected by the new authority. Vancouver Island and British Columbia became British Crown Colonies and Governor Sir James Douglas lost no time in establishing British authority over the Native people. Missionaries, determined to spread out among the Indians and Christianize them, were given the power of magistrates and Indians who seriously opposed the new regime could be thrown in jail.

One thing the newcomers would not tolerate was the Indian habit of going around in a state of near or total nudity. In those days pioneer women wore long skirts down to their ankles and it was considered downright sinful to be seen in public without some sort of modestly suitable attire. The Indians were warned against being seen by the colonists unless they dressed to standards acceptable in the Victorian era.

Yet clothing styles among the Indians of the Northwest Coast were extremely practical, and it was unfortunate for them that at that time non-Indians thought it right and necessary to cover their bodies with layers of heavy clothing. But the Indians obligingly changed and they have been wearing western style clothing ever since, except for special ceremonial occasions when traditional costumes are worn.

Salish Chief, Dominic Charlie.
Cultus Lake, B.C. (Photo: W. Jilek.)

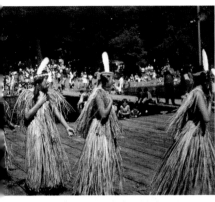

Traditional welcome dance by Stalo Indian girls in shredded bark costume.

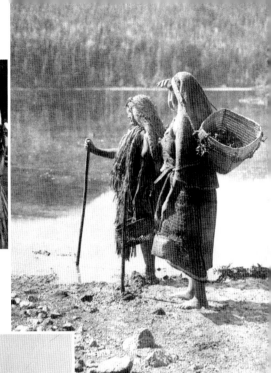

A tump line was worn across the forehead to support the weight of baskets heavy with clams.
(Photo: E.S. Curtis Collection.)

Early West Coast fisherman. Many types of spears and harpoons were used for fishing salmon, each one customized to the different fishing environments. This type of harpoon was used in deep, wide rivers, or in the sea where the salmon surface. Capes of cedar bark or cattails were worn during rainy weather.

BEAUTY CARE

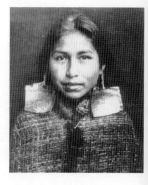

California Abalone shell earrings. California Abalone was sought after and was a popular trade item on the Northwest Coast, as the local variety was found to be too thin for inlay work or ornamentation.

A myth has been perpetuated that the North American Indian was dirty and careless about his appearance. The complete opposite was the case and the Coast Salish Indians, being a people who lived on the waterways and the seashore, were in the habit of bathing every morning as soon as they arose. They made their own soap by boiling down thimbleberry bark, and by other means such as bruising the leaves of the fragrant mock orange shrub to a soapy lather. After really dirty work, like digging in the ground for roots and bulbs or handling fish and game, they scoured themselves with cedar branches.

The Coast Salish were by necessity an outdoors people and their skin, which was a shade lighter than many tribes, glowed with health and vitality and was remarkably free from blemishes and pimples. In the pre-colonist era the Indians enjoyed a balanced diet, free from an over-abundance of starch and sugar and the results were apparent in healthy, glowing skin and strong white teeth. It has been recorded that the Nootka Indians, seeing white men for the first time after Cook's landing at Friendly Cove, were shocked by the sight of the broken, yellow teeth of the sailors and repelled by the odor of stale perspiration from the sailors' sweating, unwashed bodies.

The representative Coast Salish man was broad shouldered and sturdy, sometimes sporting a little beard and a moustache. Utilizing the two halves of a clamshell, he plucked his eyebrows into a fine line and kept his beard trimmed and tidy.

The Coast Salish, like other Northwest Coast Indian tribes, had strong and definite ideals of beauty. Tiny babies had their limbs constantly rubbed to keep them straight, the little noses were pinched to make them high and thin, and the ears encouraged to lay flat and close to the head. A flattened forehead, with the head sloping upward to the crown, was considered a mark of beauty. A pad, usually of cedar bark, was attached to the baby's cradle and bound against the forehead. By slow pressure, over a period of time, the forehead was gradually flattened to the shape preferred.

Indian maidens dieted for ceremonial purposes, but also to keep themselves slim, youthful, and aristocratic looking. Women of the Quilleute band used a sunburn lotion of sea lettuce. Klallam girls ate rose hips for a sweet breath and Lummi maidens rubbed their bodies with the bedstraw plant to give themselves a sweet aromatic odor of perfume.

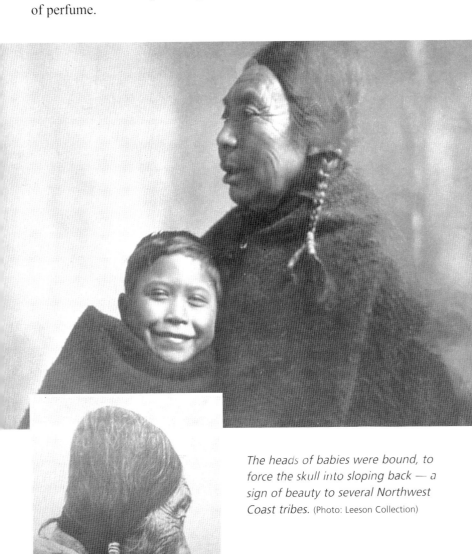

The heads of babies were bound, to force the skull into sloping back — a sign of beauty to several Northwest Coast tribes. (Photo: Leeson Collection)

FOOD

Salmon

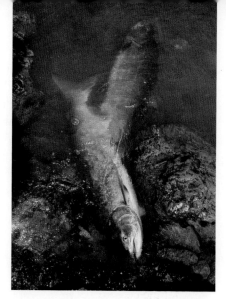

Nature set a bountiful table for the Coast Salish, as indeed for all of the Northwest Coast tribes. Salmon was by far the most important source of food, and was as basic a food to the Coast Salish as is bread to European cultures. The salmon, along with the many other varieties of fish found in both fresh and salt water, and seasonally abundant shellfish, formed the basis of the Indians' diet.

To the Native people the salmon were not really fish at all, but people living in a great magic wooden house under the sea. Every summer they sent their young men and women, disguised as fish, to meet the Native people and to provide their food. When a salmon was caught and eaten, it immediately took form again in the home village.

According to Indian legend there were five tribes of salmon, all living in a great longhouse under the sea. We know these five tribes under the names chinook (spring), sockeye (red), coho (silver), humpback (pink), and dog (chum). Each salmon tribe had its own breeding places and habits, and their behavioral patterns were as familiar to the Native people as the coming of the seasons.

For the Coast Salish, the coming of the first spring salmon was the most important event in the year. The salmon had to be treated with proper respect, and each Indian band had its own ceremony for cleaning and cooking the fish, based on age-old directions given by the salmon people themselves.

The Indians believed the first spring salmon to be the scout for the entire salmon village, and if he was not treated properly the salmon people might be offended and decide to stay away. The man

who caught him treated him almost reverently, laying him down carefully with his head upstream, so that the run would follow. Then he took the salmon home to his wife and summoned the village.

A "first salmon" ceremony followed in which rigid rules of procedure were followed. The fish was first cleaned with fern leaves; it was then cut with an ancient knife of stone or mussel shell, with the cuts made up and down, not crosswise. The fish was usually cut down the backbone, which was removed with the head on it, and the fish opened out. Then short sticks were placed across it to stretch it flat and it was roasted on a split stick before the fire. Sometimes the salmon was broken up with the hands and then boiled. The ritual included taking a piece of this first salmon and finishing eating it before sundown.

After the ceremonies in the villages were over and the run really began, everyone worked hard to harvest the salmon. While the men and boys fished and gathered wood, the women were kept busy drying the fish on long frames over smoking fires. The fish were caught with traps, spears, and nets, with each village studying its own stream and using the devices best suited to that kind of water, whether shallow or deep, swirling or clear. If a stream was shallow and clear, a favorite method was to build a weir or fence across it. The men stood on platforms along the top of the weir and scooped up the fish with long handled nets as they swarmed against the obstruction.

After the salmon was thoroughly smoked and dried — a long and tedious process — it was carefully stored away in bales or in the woven baskets Native women made for that purpose.

Weirs are used to block salmon migration, allowing the fish to be easily speared. When enough fish are caught, some woven panels are removed to let the fish swim upstream.

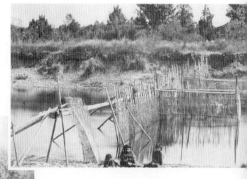

(Photos: Museum of Man
National Museum of Canada)

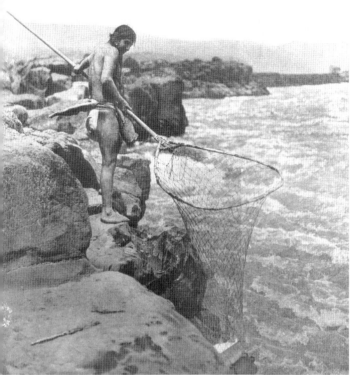

A Wishham dip net. Dip netting in pools. Denver Public Library, Western History department.

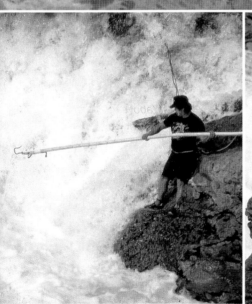

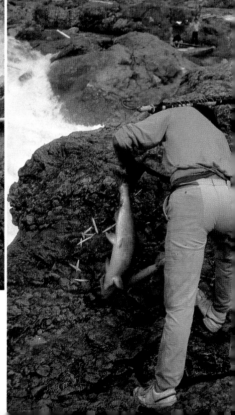

Gaff hook fishing was common along the Fraser River Canyon. Yale, B.C.

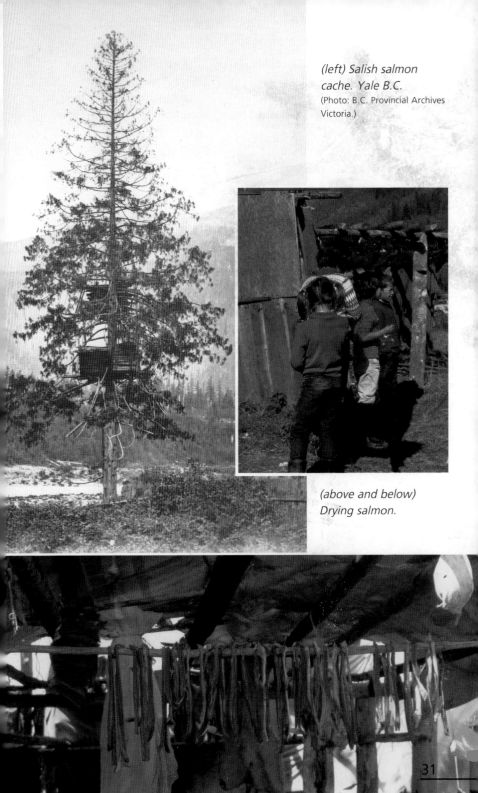

(left) Salish salmon cache. Yale B.C.
(Photo: B.C. Provincial Archives Victoria.)

(above and below) Drying salmon.

31

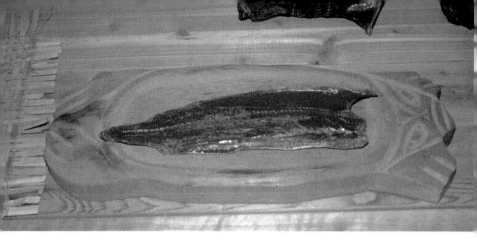

Animal figures on Salish ceremonial dishes, as on all utensils, were not crest emblems in association with any particular family. The platter in the photo is carved in the shape of a frog. When eating, one used their fingers for solid food. Wooden, or goat and sheep horn spoons were used for stews. Water was provided before and after a meal for hand washing, shredded cedar bark, used as the hand towel. *Xa:ytem Native Heritage Centre*

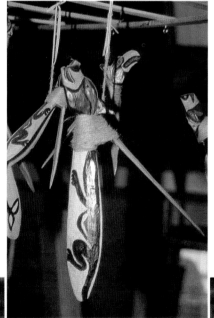

Codfish lure. This lure would be pushed down into deep water with a pole. The pole would then be removed, allowing the lure to slowly spin to the surface — the curious codfish unable to resist following it. When the fish reached the surface, it was either speared or scooped up in a dip net. Lures by artist Simon Charlie.

(below) Salmon with an eagle on top, carved by Coast Salish artist, Simon Charlie.

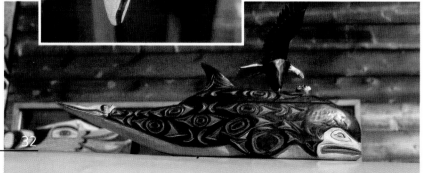

Cod, Halibut, and Sturgeon

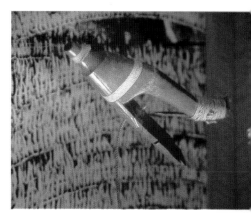

Halibut hook. Prince Rupert Museum. The carving on the halibut hook represents the spirit helper of the fisherman. Occupations such as canoe making, mountain goat hunting, or halibut fishing were considered so specialized that success in those fields could only be obtained though the help of a powerful spirit.

The Coast Salish utilized a particularly interesting method for catching cod. They made a shuttlecock device that was lowered into the water on weights and then freed by means of a trip. The cod, fascinated by the whirling motion of the device, followed its rise to the surface and were speared by the waiting fishermen. Early fur traders and settlers used to marvel at the deadly accuracy with which the Indians aimed their spears.

Halibut were regularly caught on U-or V-shaped hooks made of bent hemlock root or yew wood and attached, usually in pairs, one to each end of a slender rod four or five feet long, with the main fishing line attached to its center.

Giant sturgeon were taken from the Fraser and Squamish Rivers during spawning season. To locate the fish, the Indians used long-handled harpoons fitted with detachable heads to which were attached independent lanyards and floats. Once the position of the fish had been marked, further strikes could be made until the number of lines was sufficient to stand the strain of hauling the catch to the surface. The lines were made from dried kelp, which could be found in single strands up to 150 feet in length and had great strength after being stretched and treated.

Shellfish

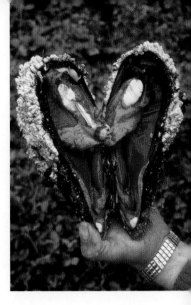

Mussel (Mytilus californianus). *This type of large sea mussel was a Nootka trade item, used to make sharp butchering blades. Clams, mussels, and other shellfish were a staple in the Coast Salish diet.*

Shellfish has been a food of the coastal tribes for thousands of years. Rock oysters, abalone, mussels, and even the barnacles found on the rocks at low tide, added to the supply of seafood.

But chief of all the shellfish was the clam, found in at least six varieties, such as rock clam, razor clam, bent nose, butter clam, cockle clam, and horse clam. Along the beaches of the Northwest Coast where Indian villages were located there are great banks, sometimes running for miles, containing stratum after stratum of clamshells, indicating century upon century of accumulation.

There is a legend that Raven, when he was a mischievous slave, stole the South Wind's daughter, thus forcing him to stop sending storms, for these storms drove the tide too far up the beach and the clams could not be uncovered.

Coast Salish women used open workbaskets for clam gathering; this allowed the water to drip out, making the load lighter and easier to carry home. The women gathered the clams just as they gathered berries and dried them by the bushel for winter use.

The "clambake" style of steaming the clams is an Indian invention. The Coast Salish dug a hole in the ground, floored it with stones, and then built a fire on them. When the fire had burned out and the stones were thoroughly hot, the clams, still in their shells, were placed upon them and covered with earth or seaweed. The clams were allowed to steam in their own juice for an hour, and by that time the shells had opened with the heat. The clams were then picked out and those not eaten immediately were impaled on skewers and hung in the sun to dry before being stored for winter use.

Clams were an important item of trade with inland people, the women eagerly trading good bags and baskets for them.

Sea Mammals

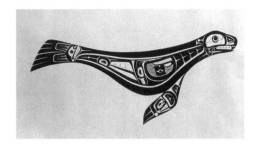

Seal by Nootka artist, Ron Hamilton.

Unlike the Nootka and Makah, famed for their courageous exploits as whalers, the Coast Salish did not systematically hunt huge sea mammals, which in any case were only rarely found in the straits. The Salish hunted smaller mammals, such as seals and porpoises, which were abundant and their flesh greatly prized.

Hunting the mammals was the privilege of the higher ranks of Salish society. The hunt required superior nerve and skill and was regarded as a task involving much honor. The hunters bathed before they went out and engaged in religious preliminaries, sanctioning their proposed undertaking by the granting of spirit power to guide them on their dangerous mission.

The smaller sea mammals did not fight like whales, and a three-man canoe, with harpooner, float man, and steersman, was all that was required for a successful hunt. The mammal was stabbed, and when tired was hauled in on the harpoon line and clubbed to death.

Another method of hunting seals was to trap a herd on shore by means of large sinew nets, stretched between rocks at a point where the seals were in the habit of taking to the water. Many of the confused mammals were clubbed to death before the herd could make its escape in another direction.

The heavy sea lion was a dangerous challenge and was the prey of only the more intrepid hunters. The meat of a seven hundred pound sea lion was sufficient to feed a whole village. The stomach could be used as a large bottle. The intestines, when twisted and dried, made tough and elastic bow strings.

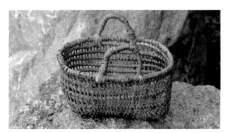

Clam Basket: No one on the coast could starve if they had access to the beach to collect clams and mussels. Collectively, these were more important than salmon.

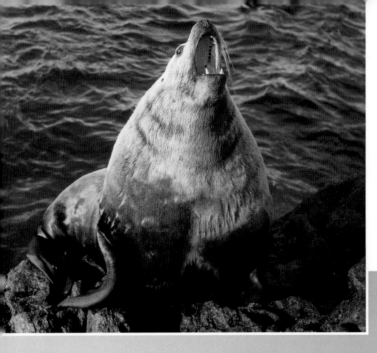

Steller Sea Lions

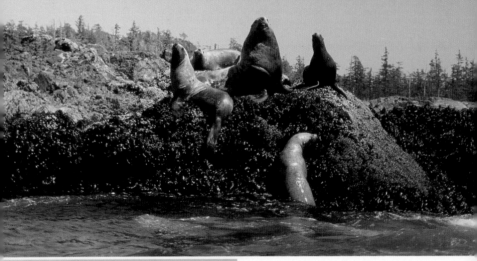

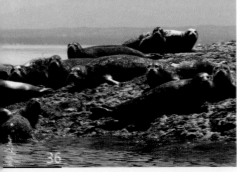

Seal hunters could mimic the cries and calls of the seal. Armed with harpoons and clubs, they would stealthily approach seals at night or in the early morning. Their canoes were equipped with specialized paddles that were designed to be quieter.

Harbor seals.

Sea Otter

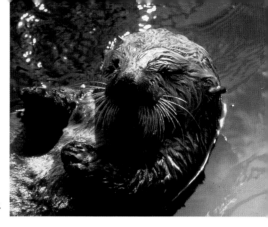

Sea otter.

Legend has it that the sea otters were the richest of the magic people who lived under the sea. The handsome young chief of their village had come one day and courted an Indian maiden. He was dressed in soft and beautiful furs and she did not know who he was. When he took her in his arms and embraced her she felt wet and cold all over. Nevertheless, she married him and her family spread blankets like carpets under her feet as she walked down to the sea. She stepped into her canoe, which was piled with wedding gifts, and the shocked watchers saw the canoe suddenly pulled down out of sight beneath the waves. Later, she returned to the village with her baby, but she was turning into a sea otter. At last, the family advised her never to come again, as she had become more otter than woman.

The sea otters did indeed have something like a village in the sea. The females bore their young on rafts of kelp where they could be seen nursing their babies, playing and diving in the waves, sitting up to eat a sea urchin held in their forepaws or merely sleeping on their backs in the waves, their little forepaws folded across their breast.

Sea otters, which are relatives of the mink and weasel, have fur so soft that the Indians called it by the word they later used to describe velvet. Wealthy indeed was the man who could afford to wear a mantle of the delicately luxurious sea otter fur. A man would trade two of his slaves for a single skin which could be cut up for use as a handsome headband, or trim to enhance a mantle of cedar bark.

Yet in Indian days sea otter hunts were only occasional affairs. When fur traders saw the commercial possibilities of sea otter pelts the unfortunate mammals were doomed. With skins selling in London for $300 each — an enormous sum in the 19th century —

the traders soon took over the hunting. They did not bother with canoes and harpoons but erected lookouts on the shore on a tripod sixty feet high. The hunter — or otter murderer as he was known — sat with a long-range gun, like a miniature cannon, and shot at every furry head that appeared. Later he went out in his boat and gathered up the bodies.

The sea otter, after near extinction along the southern coast, has been re-introduced in smaller numbers from surviving stocks in Alaska, however, it remains a threatened species.

Cougar

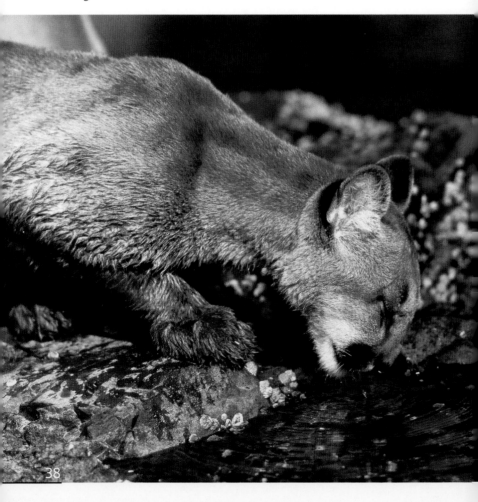

Land Mammals

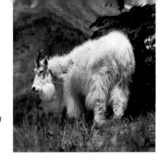

Mountain goat. The Coast Salish valued the wool of the mountain goat for the weaving of blankets.

The Indians did not traditionally hunt young fawns or any animals not yet full-grown. They believed that all animals must be allowed to grow and have young up to the height of their powers.

Deer, elk, and bear meat were a welcome addition to the Coast Salish diet, but most of all the Indians wanted the skins. Elk skin was tough enough to turn an arrow and was often used as armor in battle. Deerskin was used as wrapping material for bundles carried in canoes or stored on shelves. Bearskins were large enough to wear as mantles, without any sewing involved. Sinews could be used for fastenings, bones were a necessity for pointed tools, and teeth could be worn as ornamental jewelry or used as dice in gambling games.

Although a few brave men were trained to enter the deep forest and hunt, the Coast Salish hesitated to track game through a pathless wilderness of deadfalls and dense undergrowth. Sometimes a deer or an elk would wander on to a beach near a coastal village. Then the people would band together to chase it into the water while

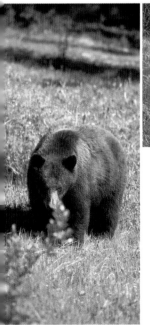

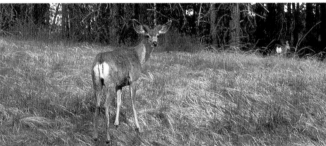

(above) Deer could be called by blowing though a blade of grass, however this was done cautiously, as a hungry cougar could be summoned instead.

(left) Black bear. When a bear's body was brought into the house it was sprinkled with down feathers and treated as an honored guest. It was believed that such courtesies would be noted by the animal's spirit and it would, in return, encourage others of its species to give themselves to the hunters.

39

a few of the men leaped hastily into canoes, armed with clubs or bows and arrows. While the unfortunate animal swam about, not knowing which way to turn, it was shot or clubbed to death.

The Puget Sound people were especially fortunate with this method, for the Sound is full of islands and animals often swam to them from the mainland. Sometimes, old timers say, a deer would swim around to scare the ducks, just for fun. If this happened while the men were away, it did not deter the womenfolk. They would jump into the canoes, and armed only with their digging sticks, manage the kill by themselves.

But the usual method for capturing and killing large game was the use of traps. Traps have been used by man down through the ages, even when he had only sticks or clubs, and the trap is probably as old a device as the net.

Modern man thinks of the trap as a devilish device with steel teeth and a steel spring. The Indians used the natural spring in a strong young sapling, bent to the ground and ready to snap back when released. A noose would be tied to such a bent tree and arranged to lie on the ground among the leaves. The bent sapling would, of course, be standing close to a deer trail. When a deer happened to step in the noose, a triggering device was released, allowing the sapling to snap back, thus jerking the noose tightly around the animal's leg.

Another plan was to dig a pit in the trail and cover it lightly with sticks and leaves. These pits were perhaps fifteen feet across and so deep that any animal falling into one would suffer serious injury. Sometimes there was a double arrangement of a pit combined with a noose.

The brown or black bear, not so fierce as a grizzly and living mostly on berries and spawning salmon, was also a frequent victim of ingenious Coast Salish trapping methods. The trapper baited the deadfall with a salmon tied with a string under a carefully balanced set of heavy logs. When the unfortunate bear jerked the salmon the heavy log, sometimes supporting the weight of other logs leaning against it, crashed down on him, injuring him severely or perhaps killing him outright.

Beavers, raccoons, cougars, bobcats, weasels, mink, and rabbits — all were caught with the hunter's trap. The secret was to know the game paths used by the animals on their way to drink at some favorite pool or stream.

Salish Dogs

Little has been recorded about the Northwest Coast Indians' dogs. Seeing hunting dogs in Indian villages was certainly a surprise to early explorers, for such a sight was rare among any of the other Indian tribes in North America.

According to the reports of early travelers, the dogs had the appearance of coyotes. They were highly trained by their masters, who called them by name, treated them like respected members of the family, and according to tales old Indians tell, even sang to them.

The dogs were trained to enter the woods and chase the game out to the hunter. The Coast Salish used them particularly for driving mountain goats into ambush and for herding deer and elk into lakes, where they could be attacked and slain by men in canoes.

What breed were these dogs? They have long since mixed with the of settlers and reliable identification is no longer possible.

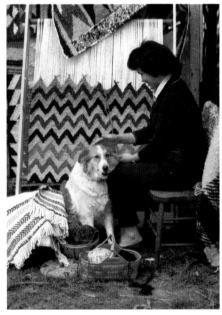

Salish weaver with her dog. Dogs that were thought to be rather like Pomeranians in appearance were domesticated and kept in small herds by select groups of Coast Salish. The hair was shorn from these dogs and used as a weaving material in conjunction with mountain goat and sheep wool, their fleece being a scarce resource.

Birds

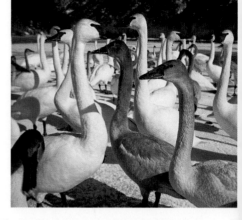

Swans

The Coast Salish knew the fly-ways along which flocks of mallard, teal, canvas back, and other varieties of duck passed. The natives set up pairs of poles, perhaps forty feet high, and between them they strung nets so fine as to be almost invisible to the naked eye. In the half-light of dawn or twilight, the unwary birds flew straight into them, and the waiting Indians were there to wring their necks.

Sighting these net poles for the first time, explorer Captain George Vancouver mistook them for flagpoles, not realizing that the Indians did not raise flags.

Many other varieties of birds flew north over the skyways. Plovers came from the South Pacific, and big white geese came down from the Arctic to enjoy the mild winter. The Indians knew the habits and seasons for each and for each they had their traps and nets ready.

The birds' flesh was a welcome change from fish. The brightly feathered skins could be sewn together and worn as mantles, used as blankets, or worn as decorative finery.

Sea birds, gulls, and their eggs were also an important food resource. Individual bands owned the offshore bird-nesting colonies, and the birds and eggs were harvested annually for their own use as well as for trade items.

Tufted puffin.

Cormorants
(Photo: Maria Krakowiak)

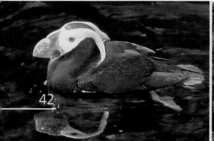

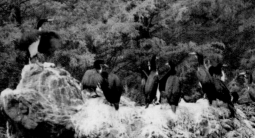

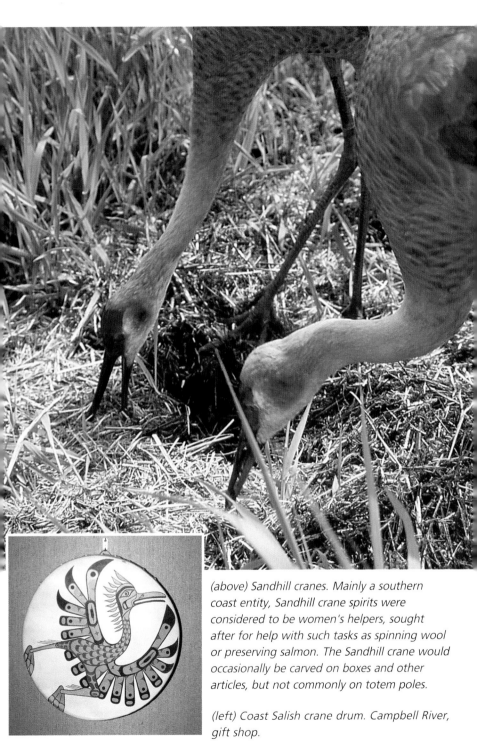

(above) Sandhill cranes. Mainly a southern coast entity, Sandhill crane spirits were considered to be women's helpers, sought after for help with such tasks as spinning wool or preserving salmon. The Sandhill crane would occasionally be carved on boxes and other articles, but not commonly on totem poles.

(left) Coast Salish crane drum. Campbell River, gift shop.

Roots and Berries

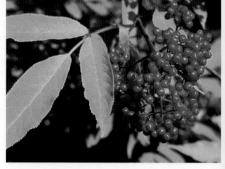

Red elder berries.

With such a bountiful harvest of edible roots, bulbs, fruits, berries, green leaves, and seaweed provided by nature for the taking, the Coastal Indians watched with awe and dismay as the early settlers cleared the land and planted vegetable gardens which successfully grew corn, peas, carrots, onions, lettuce, cabbages, and other varieties of vegetables.

To the Indians this mass clearing, leaving nothing but bare earth, was an ugly desecration. To the colonists, arable unfilled land was wasted land. Some of the settlers had endured hardships to come to this new land and gain the privilege of tilling the soil. They knew that an acre sown to wheat and potatoes would support as many people as twenty acres of hunting land. They neither knew nor cared that the fresh greens and berries growing in such wild profusion were as nourishing as the cultivated fare.

Yet even for the Indians, food gathering could involve a lot of hard work. When the long winters were over and the first green shoots of horsetail rush, cow parsnip, black cap, and salmonberry became edible, the Natives — weary no doubt of their winter diet of dried food and fish oil — ate them raw; some were so tender they needed no preparation. Others, such as salmonberry and cow parsnip, needed to have the outer bark stripped off.

The Coast Salish favored the bulbs of the camas, a lily variety, and relative of the onion, which spread its sky-blue flowers abundantly over open, grassy areas. They waited until August when the flowers had gone to seed and the plants had shriveled, and then the women went out to dig the bulbs.

Berry drying frame with cakes of red elder berries.
(Photo: Museum of Man and Nature)

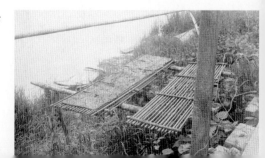

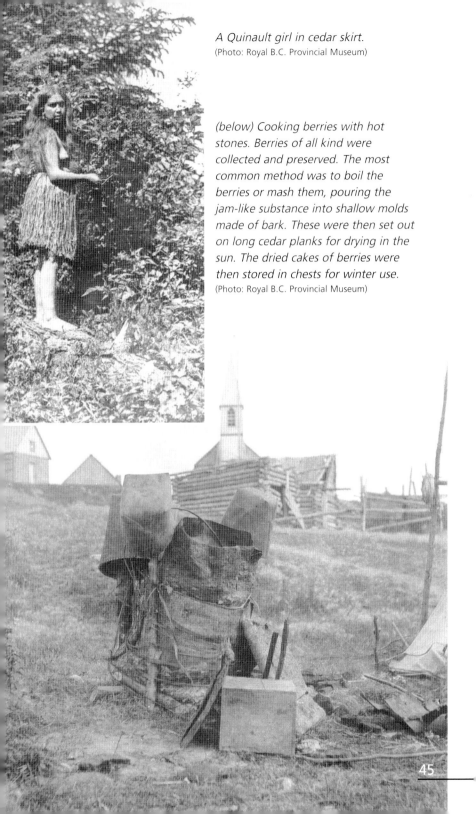

A Quinault girl in cedar skirt.
(Photo: Royal B.C. Provincial Museum)

(below) Cooking berries with hot stones. Berries of all kind were collected and preserved. The most common method was to boil the berries or mash them, pouring the jam-like substance into shallow molds made of bark. These were then set out on long cedar planks for drying in the sun. The dried cakes of berries were then stored in chests for winter use.
(Photo: Royal B.C. Provincial Museum)

Digging Sticks

Breaking sod with nothing but a pointed stick could be back-breaking work. The sticks or tools for digging were usually made of tough spruce wood with carved and pointed ends. The sticks for digging shellfish were scooped, with pointed ends to facilitate the digging, whereas the sticks for roots were less elaborate, with a slightly curved and pointed end and a simple handle for gripping.

In the case of the camas lily, they dug a trench around an entire clump of plants and then took up the whole thing, shaking the earth back into the hole and placing the bulb roots in the carrying basket.

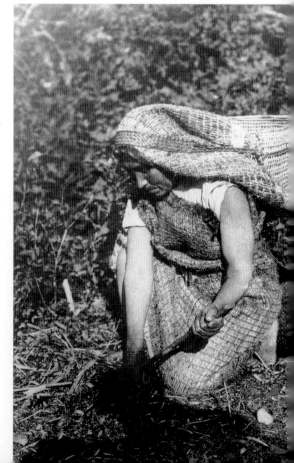

1915 photo of a woman digging roots. Coast Salish women would carefully mark the location of some plants such as the blue flowered camas lily because when the plant shrivels away in August, its bulbs are indistinguishable from another related lily that is poisonous.
(Photo: E.S. Curtis)

COOKING METHODS

Cooking methods among the Indians of the Northwest Coast were not dissimilar to those of modern times: boiling, baking, and broiling. Broiling was the favored way of cooking fresh foods. The Coast Salish gathered a few green sticks with pointed ends on which fresh fish or strips of meat could be propped before the embers of an outdoor fire and cooked to a turn. The Indians enjoyed meat and fish without salt.

Boiling was an indoor method, used in the cooking of dried foods in the long house during the winter months. Northwest Coast Indians had no metal pots and did not attempt to boil water over an open fire. The fire was used to heat stones, which were then dropped into a basket or wooden box containing cold water. As soon as the first stones cooled, they were removed and new ones added until the water boiled.

The baskets used as boiling pots were hard and tightly woven and when half filled with water they would not burn — unless the cook, perhaps busy with other cooking chores, forgot them and let the water boil out! Some of the old cooking baskets show scorched places on the bottoms, silent proof that the Native cooks of early times also burned their pots.

Baking or steaming food was an outdoor method of cooking which required a deep pit and might be described as an early type of slow cooker. A fire was lighted in a pit about three feet deep and rocks placed on top of the fuel. When the pit and the stones were thoroughly heated, the remnants of the fuel were removed and specially chosen green herbage placed on the hot stones. The food was carefully placed on top of this with more green leaves added to give protection and moisture. The pit would then be covered over with earth and hot embers and the food allowed to bake. Hard camas roots had to be baked in a pit of this sort for two or three days. A large roast of meat would cook in a few hours. Bundles of salmonberry shoots were ready in ten minutes.

Steaming, instead of baking, was accomplished by punching a hole through the earth covering, and pouring a little water into the pit. The steaming process was especially satisfactory for cooking tough roots.

The results were baked or steamed foods cooked to a tender succulence, with the flavor and vitamin content preserved.

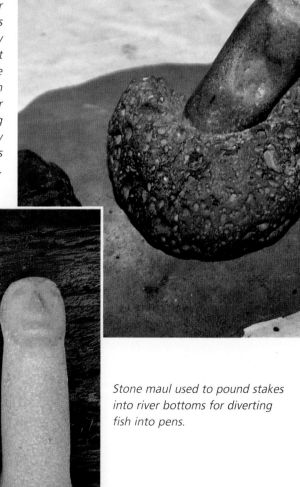

Stone bowl and grinding tool most likely used as a mortar for grinding paint pigments or dried tobacco. Nearly all recovered Northwest Coast artifacts are made of stone and have been found in the Fraser Valley, providing evidence that early culture centered in this Coast Salish region.

Stone maul used to pound stakes into river bottoms for diverting fish into pens.

CRAFTS

(below) Hat weaving form. Xa:ytem Native Heritage Centre

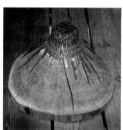

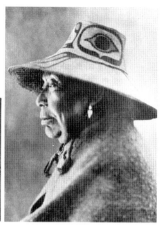

Basketry

Woman with rain hat. If a hat was worn at all, most Coast Salish people wore simple hats of bark or skins. Some groups on Vancouver Island did weave Northern-style hats, using cedar root instead of spruce root. If a wealthy person wanted a crest figure on his hat, he had to pay an artist to copy it, and for the right to use it.

Coast Salish women were famous for the high quality of their woven baskets, which were frequently adorned with beautifully imbricated designs. Each woman had three or four baskets, depending on the crops she wished to pick, and the basket was her inseparable companion on her gathering trips. The women hung the baskets on their backs by means of a woven tumpline that passed across their foreheads. For carrying clams the Coast Salish used open workbaskets that would drain the salt water. For roots they might use the same, but usually a basket with a slightly tighter weave was preferred. Tightly coiled baskets were used for berries, which are heavy when picked in quantity.

The Coast Salish women made their baskets during the long winter, but the tedious and time-consuming process of gathering and preparing materials had to be done in the summertime when the spruce and cedar roots and grasses were at their best. Roots and twigs had to be soaked, peeled and split, and grasses had to be cured and sometimes dyed.

"When I begin to weave a basket," remarked one Indian lady, "My work is already half done."

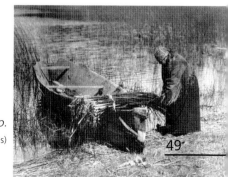

"The Tule Gatherers," 1910 E.S. Curtis photo.
(Photo: Royal B.C. Archives)

49

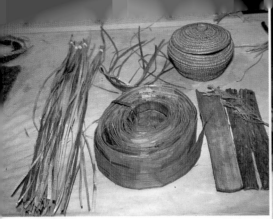

Basket-making materials. Xa:ytem Native Heritage Centre

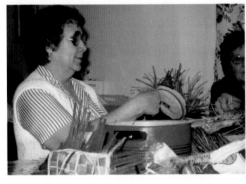

(above) Fran Edgar of Nit'Nat, weaving a basket. Lake Cowichan. (Photo: Sonia Bokic.)

(right) Coast Salish weaver.

(below) Fran Edgar of Nit'Nat.
(Photo: Sonia Bokic.)

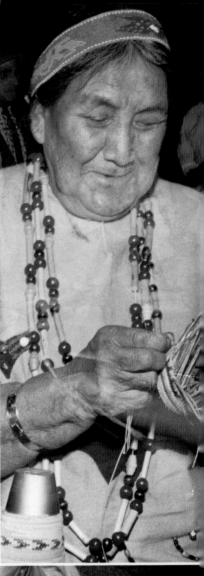

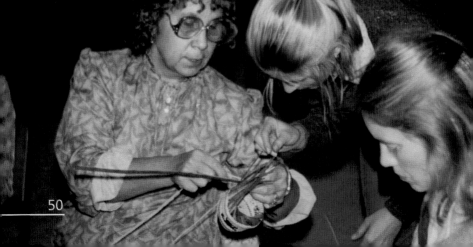

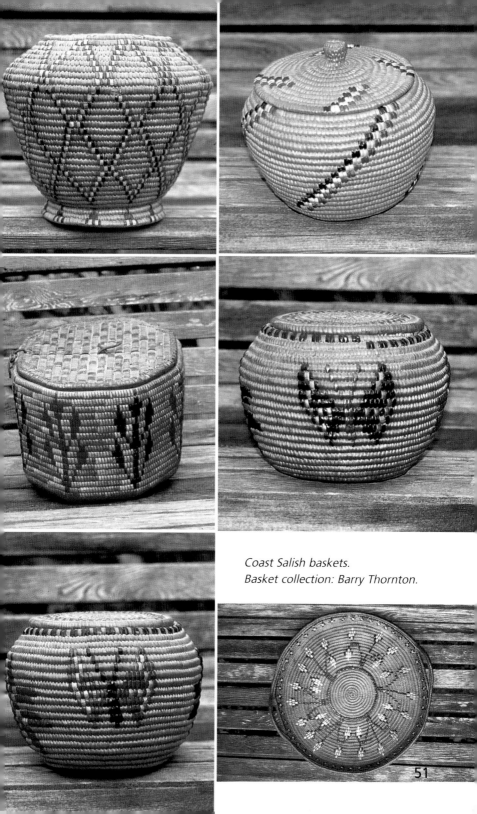

Coast Salish baskets.
Basket collection: Barry Thornton.

Depending upon final use, weaving methods were subject to considerable variation, with the woven basketry developing in twined and twilled forms. Twined work took the form of soft-rush bags and openwork, useful for carrying roots or clams and, on a larger scale, for the manufacturing of fish traps. Twilled products, on the other hand, generally took the form of pouches, sewing baskets, or hold-alls.

The heavy coiled baskets were known as "hard baskets" and were woven by an entirely different method. In this construction the foundation strands go around the basket, not up and down. They are coiled around in a spiral, and each is sewn to the one below it by means of vertical stitches, passing over the upper strand and under or through the lower. Bone awls were used as needles and the stitching was of threads of roots or grass. The part of the coil being sewn was pressed together with the fingers while the binding strand was pulled tight with the teeth. So tightly were these baskets sewn that when soaking swelled them they became completely watertight.

Decorating the coiled baskets was done by a clever process termed imbrication. Bear grass was the favored decorating material but it was fragile as straw and, used alone, could not have held a basket together. Either strips of this glossy grass or dyed bark were overlapped upon the overcast stitching which binds the coils of the "hard basket" together. A row of it, pleated under the sewing stitches around a basket, looked something like a row of shingles, overlapping at the side instead of the top and bottom.

One of the most common and best loved designs was done in a deep V pattern and is believed by some women to represent the waves in a lake, the idea for the design having come to a basket weaver in ancient times in the form of a vision. Another popular design was a series of diagonal lines zigzagging around the basket in harmonious forms, which some Indians say were originally inspired by lightning storms.

The old baskets, still beautiful and with age adding a soft patina to the imbrication, are much sought after as historic works of art by museums, and by collectors who admire them for the sheer artistry of weave and design.

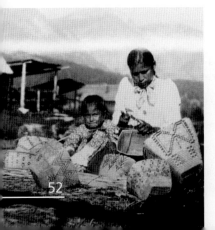

Salish weaver. Fine quality baskets with imbrications of dark cherry bark.
(Photo: Royal B.C. Archives.)

Weaving

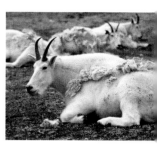

Shedding mountain goat. Much of wool used by Coast Salish weavers was collected from the ground and off the bushes that shedding goats had passed by. Additional fibers such as fireweed, dog hair, and duck down were often added to supplement the wool.

Coast Salish women, using a simple loom, wove in wool — a practice uncommon in early North America since the continent was not well supplied with wool-bearing animals until after the introduction of sheep by settlers.

The Coast Salish used the wool of the mountain goat. The Salish Indians along the Fraser River sometimes hunted the goats and traded the hides to the coast. They also searched over the hillsides in spring and summer when the goats were shedding, and gathered the tufts of fur which rubbed off on the bushes as the animals passed by. Perhaps it was this gift of wool that inspired Salish women to begin weaving cloth.

But the Puget Sound women had their own little wool-bearing animal — a tame dog, quite small, but with a thick coat of creamy wool which could be shorn at regular intervals. When the wool was hacked off with a mussel shell knife, the fleece was so thick that, according to one historian, you could lift it up by one corner, like a mat.

Early explorers describe the dogs as having the appearance of Pomeranians, usually white in color, but sometimes varying to a brownish black. They were usually kept on tiny islands in Puget Sound and the Strait of Juan de Fuca and were not found among the more northerly Indians of the Northwest Coast.

The women would paddle out daily from the village with food and drink for the dogs and always took them along with them during prolonged absences from the village on food gathering trips and

Spinning, goat's wool.
(Photo: Royal B.C. Provincial Museum)

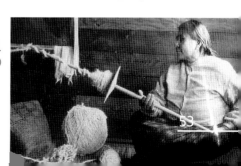

other necessary excursions. It was said that the number of dogs she owned judged a woman's wealth.

Captain George Vancouver reported meeting a group of two hundred Indians, most of them in canoes, but a few walking along with a drove of about forty dogs that were sheared close to the skin like sheep.

The wool of the dogs was much finer than that of the goats, and the yarns produced from it were very much like those of a fine grade, commercial wool. The shearing was sometimes repeated two or three times in a summer and even then it was hard to get enough wool for many blankets.

Women would mix the dog wool with mountain goat wool, goose or duck down, and the cotton from the fireweed and other plants, in any proportions available. Clay beaten into the wool with a flat, sword-like piece of wood helped remove the grease from the wool and also whitened it, for dog wool was not as white as the wool of the mountain goat.

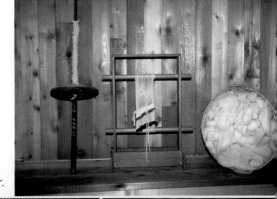

(right) Spindle whorl, loom and bail of goat wool.

(below, left) Salish weaver.

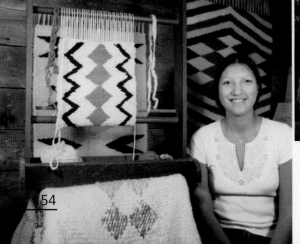

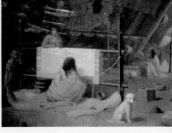

(above) Artist, Paul Kane's painting of a Salish two-bar loom, and a wool dog.

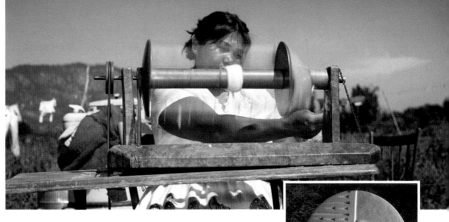

(above) Spinning wool.

(right) Large whorls, such as this one that was carved by Herb Cook, were used exclusively by the Coast Salish. They were used to keep the wool from falling off the spindle while spinning yarn by hand.

Next the weaver combed the fibers out with her fingers or hand carders and then rolled them on her leg. The wool was then ready for spinning. The spindle used was a smooth stick three or four feet long. At its lower end was the whorl of carved wood (often beautifully decorated) that kept the strands from slipping.

The loom for weaving the yarn consisted of two horizontal rollers supported in slots cut in wooden uprights set in the ground. Although not always used, the alternate strands of the warp were often kept apart by a simple heddle of thin wood to allow the hand to pass through. The warp was run around these rollers in a series of continuous cords so that the web could frequently be pulled around to a convenient position for the weaver, who always wove from the top downwards.

The technique used in weaving the goat wool blanket could be compared to that of twilled basketry, in which the weft crosses the warp in the sequence of over two and under one.

There was little use of color until the settlers brought yarn in trade. Then a few really beautiful blankets were made in fine yarn and magnificent color.

The opening of the Hudson's Bay Company trading posts and the subsequent appearance of the easily obtainable Hudson's Bay blankets spelled the death knell for the weaving of these beautiful

Salish blankets and mantles, some which were ten or twelve feet long and were used for bedding. Smaller ones — perhaps half the length — were used as mantles. Only a few survive today in museums and private collections.

With the coming of the gold rush in 1858 and the resultant drastic changes in Coast Salish life styles, the dogs were no longer a valuable commodity and soon became extinct. Today there is not an Indian living that even remembers how they looked.

The art of weaving the Coast Salish blanket has enjoyed a dramatic revival, thanks mostly to the efforts of the late Oliver Wells who wrote the book *Salish Weaving Primitive and Modern, As Practiced by the Salish Indians of South West British Columbia* (Sardis: 1969), to renew interest in this long overlooked art. The Salish are weaving their blankets again on simple looms, just as they did more than a century ago. Beautiful natural dyes color the blankets with attractive geometric patterns; alder bark can be used for red; lichen for yellow; cedar and hemlock bark for brown; Oregon grape for a yellow-green; and copper for blue-green.

Coast Salish nobility blanket. This colorful style of blanket emerged in Coast Salish culture after English trade cloth became available. Cloth would be unraveled, or torn into small strips, then re-spun. The weaver then blended this new yarn with the goat's wool, creating a new form.

Weaver wearing a traditional Coast Salish blanket. The white fabric of blankets used to be enhanced with white clay. Dark animal hair and wools colored with organic dyes were used to create the contrasting patterns.

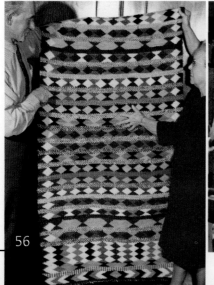

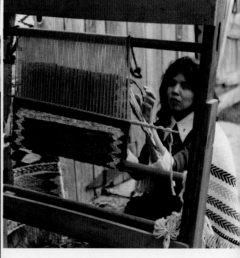

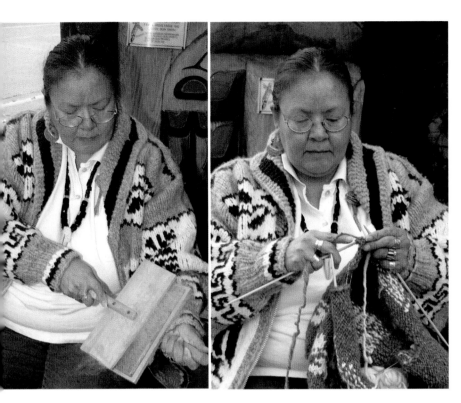

Duncan, B.C. Salish knitter, Pauline
Jo, 'carving' wool in preparation
for knitting a sweater.

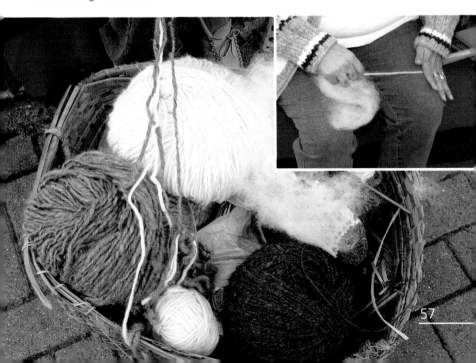

CANOES

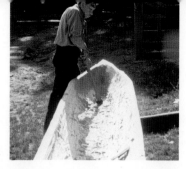

Hollowing out a canoe.

Among the Indian tribes of the northwest, travel was essentially by sea or via the inland waterways. The canoe was the Indians' only means of transportation over long distances. Without it they would have been penned up in their villages with no way to visit, hunt, trade, or go to war.

The famous, yet frail, birch bark canoes of other North American Indian tribes would have been of little use to Northwest Coast Indians in rough Pacific waters. Instead they crafted sturdy dugouts — sometimes fifty feet long and six to eight feet wide — from the trunks of cedars. Explorers Lewis and Clark reported that the largest ones could carry eight to ten thousand pounds, or twenty to thirty persons.

The Coast Salish did not traditionally build ocean-going canoes, although they were known to have traded furs for them with the Nootka on Vancouver Island. The most seaworthy of all canoes, and certainly most beautiful in form and line with their projecting bows and sterns raised high above the water, were those of the Haida.

In early times some canoes had sails made of cedar bark matting. The origin of these sails is not known. Some suggest the idea came from traders but the use of sails could have arrived long before, perhaps from the sighting of a Chinese junk wrecked in Pacific waters.

Dugout canoes were made in various shapes and sizes according to their purpose. Apart from the great sea-going canoes there were inland varieties — shorter and shallower freight canoes for river, small hunting canoes about ten feet long, and a one-man canoe used mainly for duck hunting. Then there was a kind of knock-about canoe used for sealing and, in modern times, the slim, slick ones for racing.

A common sight at an Indian village, especially one near salt water, was that of

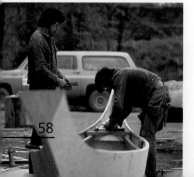

Setting in the seats.

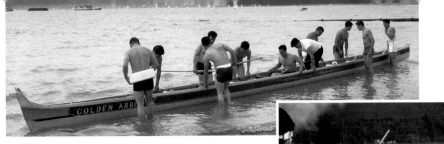

Coast Salish canoe races at Vancouver, B.C. (above) and Cultus Lake, B.C. (right).

many dugouts of various shapes and sizes, drawn up and turned over on the beach and covered with mats to protect them from the sun.

The Coast Salish honored canoe builders; there were generally only one or two such craftsmen in each village. Manufacturing the canoes was originally the work of this specialist whose work was assisted by spirit helpers. Because of this belief, special rites were conducted, songs were sung, and taboos observed by the builder and his wife during the period of construction. This privacy was especially insisted upon during the more critical phases, such as the first splitting of the log and the steaming and spreading of the sides.

The log had not only to be hollowed out, but also to be shaped and curved. For this the canoe maker used what might almost be described as cooking methods. A fire was lit around the outside of the canoe at a distance that would heat the wood without scorching it. The canoe, roughly shaped and hollowed out by means of splitting off slabs with wedges, was then almost filled with water that was heated with hot stones. At this point the skill and experience of the canoe maker was put to its greatest test.

When the canoe was first hollowed out, the bottom was deliberately left bellied up in the center, and a similar line allowed to the gunwales. This form allowed for spreading, a process which

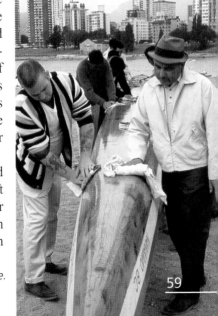

Drying a Coast Salish racing canoe.

59

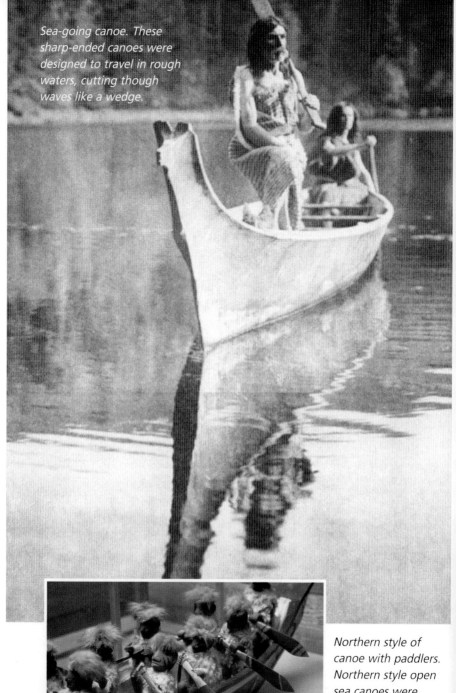

Sea-going canoe. These sharp-ended canoes were designed to travel in rough waters, cutting though waves like a wedge.

Northern style of canoe with paddlers. Northern style open sea canoes were purchased in trade on occasion. Prince Rupert Museum.

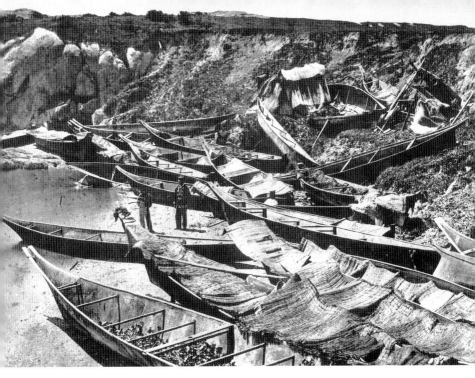

Salish canoes near Victoria, circa 1870. (Photo: Royal B.C. Provincial Archives)

Puget Sound canoe. The Coast Salish designed smaller canoes for sheltered water. They were used for short trips, such as local fishing and sealing. (Photo: E.S. Curtis)

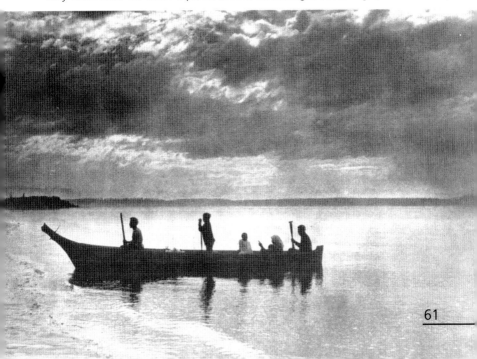

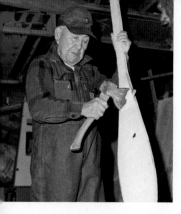

Richard Harry carving a paddle. (Photo: J. Ralph)

could add as much as two feet to the original width of the log. Thus a log three feet in width might become a canoe with a five-foot beam.

Between the warm fire and the steaming process, the wood fibers became soft and pliable. The builder meanwhile cut stout pieces of yew wood just the width the canoe would have at various points along its length. At the center, of course, it would be considerably wider than the original log, while it would taper at both ends. The sticks of yew wood were wedged between the gunwales, like thwarts, so that the sides were kept bulging. Then the water was dipped out and the canoe left to dry in its curved shape.

The fine work was done by patiently charring with fire, controlled by damp sand, and then hacking off the charcoal with an adze. The D-adze was used for the final shaping, and even finer work was done with chisels held in elk-horn handles. Further sanding of surface areas was accomplished by rubbing with the rough part of a dogfish skin.

The Indians of the Northwest Coast often painted their canoes with exciting designs representing creatures of the sea such as killer whales or sharks, and even birds and animals. Among the more southerly tribes, paint was sparse and only two colors were used. The inside of the canoe was usually colored red. The Indians made a sort of oil paint by mixing red ochre with fish or seal oil, just as modern paint is mixed with linseed oil. The outside of the canoe was first smoothed with sharkskin and then charred lightly with a cedar bark torch. This singed off the roughness and left the canoe a dull black.

The thwarts were fastened tightly to the sides of the canoe by cedar withes passed through holes in thwart and gunwale. Paddlers had to sit, or kneel, or lean against them and since they were round poles, they were never very comfortable unless cedar bark mats were folded over them as a kind of padding.

Paddles were carved from yew or maple wood and polished smooth with sharkskin. Some paddles were pointed at the end so they could be dug into the beach to hold the canoe, but usually the paddle blade had a rounded end.

RELIGION

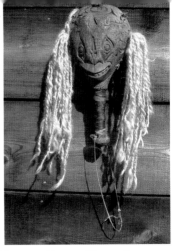

*Coast Salish shaman's rattle.
Carved by Simon Charlie.*

For the Coast Salish, as indeed with all of the Northwest Coast tribes, almost every action in life was centered on spirit power. All objects, whether animate or inanimate, contained spirits that could influence lives. Since the Natives deeply felt the influence of the unseen world in every happening, they had to constantly strive to positively influence these spirits on their behalf. Yet there was no ritualistic worship of a supreme being.

When the missionaries came and tried to wipe out Native beliefs and Christianize the Indians, they had no understanding of how deeply they were reaching into Indian moral codes and behavioral patterns. There was a mistaken belief among early missionaries that Native carving representing family crests on totem poles, welcoming figures, or other such items, in the form of animals, birds, and sea mammals, were worshiped in some form of pagan idolatry.

The Coast Salish world was filled with many spirit forms, guardian spirits, supernatural beings, transformers, and demigods endowed with various powers and jurisdictions. As with other coastal groups there was a suggestion of a "creator of the world" but his powers do not appear to have been absolute and, because of this lack of omnipotence, he frequently required aid from near equals who enjoyed concurrent jurisdiction in some areas.

Christians believe that the force of life is concentrated in one all-pervasive God residing in the heavens. The Coast Salish, like most North American Indians, were more inclined to think of life's force as pervading the world like an electric current. This power might show itself in almost anything, from the cry of the loon to a flash of lightning.

There also existed an underlying belief in the essential oneness of man with nature. Originally, according to Indian belief, all living creatures shared in a world of mutual harmony and understanding, and one at all times preserved a proper respect for the habits and dwelling places of all species of life.

This "oneness of life" philosophy led to the concept of "animal people" — beings with the characteristics of both animals and man. Strip a bird of his feathers, or the fur from a bear, or the scales from a fish and the form becomes indistinguishable from human form. Thus a deserving man might establish a close relationship with a wolf spirit who would become his helper and aid him in developing wolf power to assist him in growing to be a great hunter.

The Coast Salish believed that the soul of a man was twofold. First was that indestructible spark which, once departed, went to the sunset where it remained forever. Then that which was left behind was the earthly body and its shadows. These shadows held a three-part existence and remained on the earthly scene with either good or evil intent, depending on the character of the person in life.

Spirit dance attire. Lummi Salish. The Coast Salish believed that each person had the potential to have a spirit helper. Helping spirits were revealed to people in dream visions. These entities were desirable for the abilities that they could bestow upon the recipient. Prowess at canoe building, seal hunting, and any other occupation was considered due to supernatural intervention. During the winter months, spirit dances were held allowing people to reaffirm their connection with their personal helper spirit.

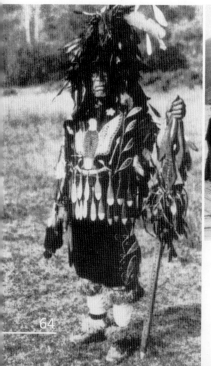

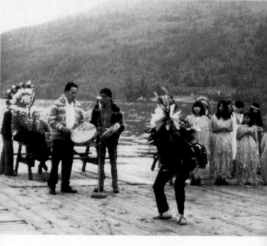

(above) Roy Point, Mit Kinder, and Tom Grappe.
(Photo: Jilek.)

64

Shaman or Medicine Man

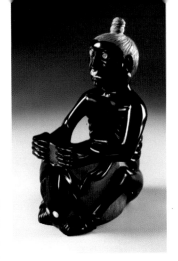

Seated Shaman's bowl by Salish artist, Luke Marston.

The shaman was a very important man in his community. He was the medicine man, the Indian equivalent of the modern doctor. Moreover, he played a leading part in all ceremonial functions and was much sought after for his help and advice in times of trouble and distress.

Early missionaries painted an unpleasant and untrue picture of the medicine man as a charlatan and a cheat. On the contrary, a shaman had a sincere belief in self and often affected remarkable cures among his people. Perhaps he practiced a form of hypnotism or used the power of suggestion on his patients, but among the Indians at least there persisted a firm belief in his powers and in his ability to cure people of sickness and suffering.

In the Coast Salish society there were two classes of shamans — those who held supreme powers in the arts of clairvoyance, curing the sick, and controlling the ghosts and shadows of men, and those of lesser powers who concerned themselves with minor illnesses and the warding off of adverse influences. The latter were usually women, who applied themselves mostly to the practice of midwifery.

The shaman was required to lead an exemplary life among his people. He was repeatedly required to give demonstrations of his powers before being accepted as a medicine man that could accept fees for his work. He had an animal "helper" who had been revealed to him in a dream during his days as a novice, and this animal became his relative and could be invoked by him at any time when assistance was needed.

The Coast Salish believed that disease originated as an evil spirit that had penetrated the body and induced pain and suffering. The shaman, performing ritualistic songs and dances and sprinkling water over the patient, attempted to draw out the evil spirit by sucking on the afflicted part. Proof of his success depended on the patient's recovery. If the sick person failed to get better, a feeling of enmity could develop toward the medicine man whose powers had failed.

The shamans attempted to keep up their prestige by staging public exhibitions. At many of the big feasts there were contests where shamans removed snakes from their bodies, or picked hot stones out of the fire and danced with them.

The life of the shaman was full of dangerous suspicions and intrigues. If too many of his patients died, the entire village might begin to fear him and conclude he was a sorcerer, with the result that someone could decide to go out and kill him as a public service.

A missionary who once witnessed a medicine man at work wrote later that he never forgot the occasion. The patient lay in a coma on rush mats inside the longhouse. The shaman had first to make a diagnosis. He went into a spirit dance calling on his spirit helper to help him "see" what was afflicting the sick man. Everyone in the village had gathered to beat on the roof with poles to help him achieve his power. The medicine man — masked and wearing a headdress of cedar bark and shaking his rattle — bounded in and danced around the patient. His helpers followed him, repeating a song until finally the shaman went into a trance, showing that his spirit was with him. When he came out of it, weary and exhausted, he had full knowledge of what was causing the patient's ailment.

Shamans were not known to get particularly rich. Why did some men choose to go through the grueling rituals of obtaining medicine power? He was something like a priest and elder statesman in his village. He was consulted on almost every occasion and commanded more obedience than the chief of the village. He was feared as well as respected, and his prominence in the village was assured.

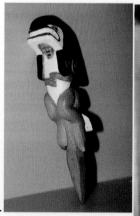 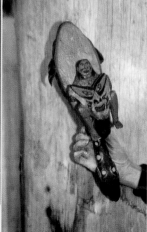

Two shaman's rattles by Simon Charlie.

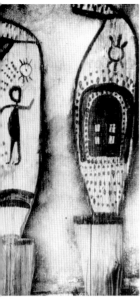

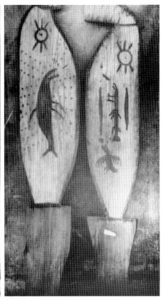

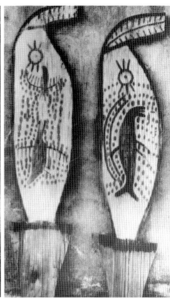

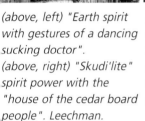

(above, left) "Earth spirit with gestures of a dancing sucking doctor".
(above, right) "Skudi'lite" spirit power with the "house of the cedar board people". Leechman.

(above left) Shamanic eye.
(above, right) "Travelers or the shaman's spirit helpers. Dots represent the power songs revealed to the shaman. 1920. Leechman.

(above, left) "Duck spirit powers swallowing illness". Illness is represented by the short line between the ducks.
(above, right) "Sxuda'te" spirit power twisting victims into knots. Leechman.

Spirit canoe planks. The Coast Salish believed that illness was caused when one's living spirit had found its way to the land of the dead. In order for the spirit be returned to the living, some Coast Salish groups believed a ritual canoe trip had to be undertaken by powerful spirit helpers. The Lummi shaman made this symbolic journey every winter on behalf of all the sick in the community. The shaman would call on those who had spirit helpers, to assist him. Each assistant brought his spirit plank (above) in order to create a formation, (below) which represented the spirit canoe. Once the canoe was assembled, the assistants would take their paddling positions, ready for the supernatural adventures ahead.

(right) Setting up spirit canoe planks. Leechman.
(Photos: Private Collection, Prof. E. Margetts. M.D.)

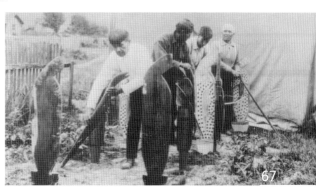

Secret Societies

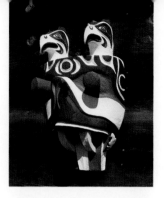

Skhway-Khwey mask, carved by Simon Charlie. These masks represented a mythical being that had descended from the sky, into the bottom of a deep lake.

For the Coast Salish, secret societies were neither as numerous nor as well organized as those of the northern tribes. It seems likely that such societies were largely the result of a culture transfer. For example, a variety of such societies existed among Coast Salish bands in close contact with the Kwakiutl. Yet farther south, in the Puget Sound and Fraser River area, secret societies were scarce and not highly regarded.

The function of these societies was basically religious, but the wildly mysterious initiation ceremonies seemed utterly pagan to early missionaries, so under the influence of the christian church, the societies either carried on in great secrecy, or died out altogether.

The spirit that inspired the society was always wild and terrifying. Usually it was some sort of cannibal monster that most tribes referred to as "black tamanous" (tah-mah-no-us) or black spirit. One could not hope to receive this spirit by merely seeking it. The initiate had also to pay high dues to the society and then be prepared to give a huge feast. This meant that only rich men's sons could join, and the society had only a few members in any one tribe. Nevertheless, a member's prestige was very high. They could, it was whispered, stand any kind of pain without feeling it. They looked so terrifying in their costumes that people obeyed them out of fear.

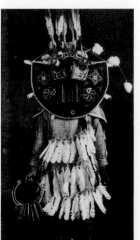

Initiation played an important part, and novices were required to be of pure mind and unimpeachable behavior. As a consequence, most of the novices were adolescents with their fathers acting as sponsors. When the probationer was granted entry into the society, he traditionally disappeared into the woods where he fasted, bathed frequently in cold water, and

1912 masked Cowichan dancer. Provincial Archives, Victoria B.C.

scrubbed himself with rough cedar bark boughs. The combination of extreme physiological deprivation and psychological preparation eventually brought about a successful outcome to the vision quest.

During the initiate's absence, his mother worked new mountain goat wool blankets for him and perhaps ornaments of cedar bark. Then when the youth returned, his father gave a five-day feast. During the feast, dances were performed to which all people were admitted. The society members occupied one side of the longhouse. Dressed in their regalia of cedar bark ornaments, their faces blackened to emphasize the solemnity of the occasion, and their hair strewn with down to indicate inward rejoicing, the members were a truly impressive sight.

At the end of the five days, the novice underwent a ceremonial bathing in the sea and again retired to the woods for further experience of privation and exposure, returning only from time to time for instruction in the rites of the society. The black spirit finally terminated the woods-dwelling period by revealing itself to the youth and becoming his guard and guiding him in all his future ways.

Having found his spirit, the novice returned triumphantly to the house where another feast, accompanied by a potlatch, was given. The time had now come for the graduate to perform his dance and reveal himself to the people as a full-fledged member of the secret society.

Most of the animal masks used by the Coast Salish on these occasions are not native to them but are borrowed from other tribes. However, one mask truly Coast Salish in origin is the remarkable skhwaykhwey mask that is still used in ceremonial dances in the Nanaimo and Cowichan area, and the adjacent mainland.

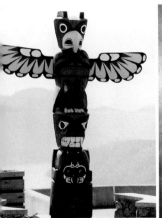 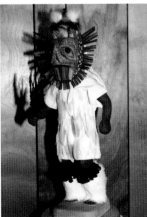

(left) A Coast Salish Thunderbird totem with a bear holding a Skhway-Khwey mask.

(right) Artist Jane Marston's carving of a Salmon Skhway-Khwey masked doll.

69

MYTHS AND LEGENDS

The Coast Salish had no written language and therefore stories of tribal origin, history, achievements, and newly learned facts had to be passed on verbally from one generation to the next through myths and legends.

Many Coast Salish myths are found among the legends of the inland plateau people — the ancestral homeland of Coast Salish. For example, the creation myth of the interior that tells of an old man who walked the earth creating the outstanding features of the landscape, or altering conditions previously established by supernatural "transformers" such as the raven and coyote, has many variations among coastal tribes.

Story telling was an essential part of the cultural heritage of the Indian. Gathered around the lodge fires during the long winter evenings, children listened to legends and myths reaching far back in Coast Salish history and young minds became a storehouse of knowledge. The stories were acted out with intense dramatic effect with the speaker waving his arms, crouching, and even changing his voice in dramatic imitations of the characters involved in his story.

Legends and myths also formed the basis for the ceremonial songs and spirit dances that took place inside the longhouses when the people gathered together for the winter ceremonies.

Early Quamichan exterior house posts. B.C. Provincial Museum.

Cowichan dance house painting by Mildred Valley Thornton.

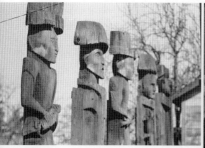
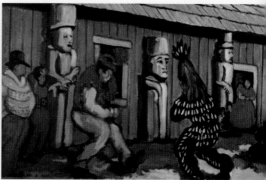

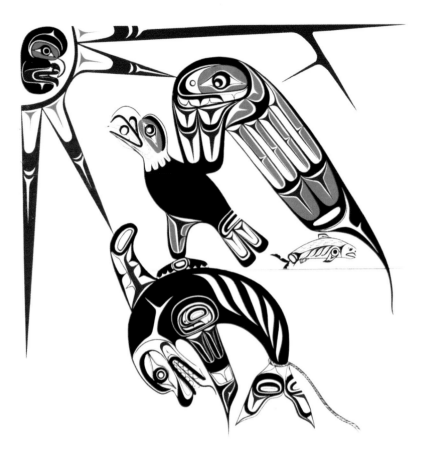

Reproduced from an original drawing by Floyd Joseph, this represents an illustration of an ancient Squamish legend "Why the salmon came to Squamish waters."

A long time ago, animals and birds and people were really the same, only disguised in different forms. The chief of the Squamish band was sad because no salmon lived in Squamish waters and sometimes the people went hungry. One day the village was visited by four brothers who possessed great supernatural powers. The sorrowing chief decided to ask the brothers for help in persuading the salmon people to swim to Squamish shores.

The four brothers, famous for their good deeds, gladly offered their services. But a problem presented itself. Where did the salmon people live? How could they be found? It was decided to ask Snookum the sun. Snookum could see all over the world from his home in the sky. But how could anyone get near enough to Snookum to ask him anything? Obviously the sun would have to be tricked into coming down to the Squamish village.

After much pondering of the matter the brothers used their great powers; the youngest of them was transformed into a salmon and then tied to the shore with a fishing line. The salmon leaped and sported in the water until he attracted the attention of Snookum. But before doing anything, the crafty sun caused the three brothers to go into a deep trance. Then, having changed himself into the form of a magnificent eagle, Snookum flew down from the sky, dug his claws into the salmon, and rose rapidly up into the heavens, breaking the line in his flight.

The brothers, upon waking from their trance, decided to try again. This time they transformed the third brother into a whale and tied him to the shore with a very strong line. For the second time, Snookum cast the brothers into a trance and descended from the sky in the form of an eagle. He landed on the floating whale and dug his claws into the flesh. At first in seemed the great sun-eagle would surely lift the the whale right out of the water. But the rope did not break and and the frantic flapping of the eagle's wings did not succeed in freeing his claws from the back of the whale.

While the struggle continued, the brothers awoke from their trance. The whale was pulled to the shore, the captured eagle still on his back. Thoroughly outwitted, the sun-eagle agreed to tell the brothers the whereabouts of the home of the salmon people in return for his release.

Snookum revealed that the salmon people lived a long distance away to the west, but cautioned that if the Squamish people desired to live with them they must first prepare much medicine and take it with them on their journey. The sun was then allowed to go and, still in eagle form—he took flight and soared away and up into the clouds back to his home in the sky.

Led by the brothers, the Squamish people paddled their canoes, traveling ever westward, until they reached the home of the salmon, where they were very cordially received. The Squamish gave some of their medicine to the chief of the village, Spring Salmon (Chief Kos), and as a result of this he was very friendly to the whole party.

In a stream which flowed in behind the village, Chief Kos, kept a fish trap. The salmon chief directed four of his young people, two boys and two girls, to enter the water and swim up the creek into the salmon-trap. Obeying his orders the young people drew their blankets up over their heads and walked into the sea. No sooner had the water lapped against their faces then they became salmon. Leaping and playing together, just as salmon do in the running season, they swam their way to the trap in the creek.

Later, when it came time to welcome the strangers with a feast, Chief Kos ordered the fish to be brought from the trap to be cleaned and roasted. The four salmon were cleaned and cut open and then spread above the flames on wooden grill.

When the chief invited his guests to eat he made a point of insisting that they must not throw away any of the bones. They were to lay them aside carefully, taking care that not even a small bone was destroyed. When the meal was over and the satisfied guests had finished eating, all the bones were carefully gathered up and thrown into the sea. A few minutes later, the four young people who had earlier entered the sea and been changed into salmon, reappeared in their original human form and waded out of the water to join the others. As a result of this strange occurrence and similar happenings, such as the time a curious guest held back some of the bones at a later feast, the Squamish became convinced that they had indeed found the home of the salmon people. This withholding of some of the bones resulted in a near disaster, with one of the youths coming out of the sea with part of his face missing and being made whole again only when the guilty Squamish youth produced the bones, pretending he had just found them.

The eldest of the four brothers explained the purpose of their visit to the salmon chief. He told how the Squamish people were often poor and hungry, and requested that salmon be allowed to visit Squamish waters and swim in the Squamish streams.

Chief Kos agreed on one condition — that the Squamish be careful with the bones and always be sure to throw them back in the water, just as they had seen the salmon people do.

"If you are careful with the bones," said Chief Kos, "my people can return to us again after they visit you."

The four brothers and the Squamish promised to adhere carefully to this rule, thanked their host, and prepared for their return journey across the water, toward the rising sun.

As they were leaving, Chief Kos called to them: "I will send spring salmon to you the first in the season. After them I will send the sockeye, then the cohoe, then the dog-salmon, and last of all the humpback."

The chief kept his word and ever since that time, so very long ago, different varieties of salmon in that order have come to the Squamish waters to help feed the people. And in the days of old, before the coming of the white people, the Indians obeyed the words of Chief Kos and were very careful to throw the salmon bones back into the water.

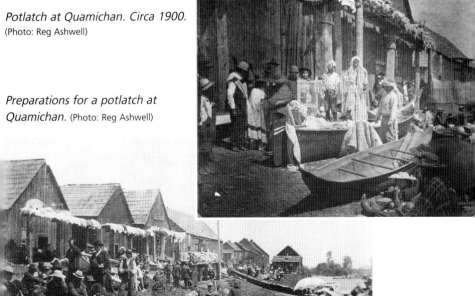

Potlatch at Quamichan. Circa 1900.
(Photo: Reg Ashwell)

Preparations for a potlatch at Quamichan. (Photo: Reg Ashwell)

POTLATCH

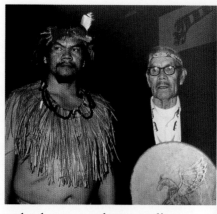

Ceremonial dancers.
(Photo: J. Ralph)

The very cornerstone of Coast Salish society was based on the potlatch, as indeed it was with all of the Northwest Coast tribes. The potlatch was a rather complicated "giving away", or redistribution of wealth, ceremony in which the recipients of lavish gifts were bound to reciprocate by inviting the donors to a return potlatch, where they had to prove their standing and influence by giving back far more than they had received. These endless potlatches, and the fantastic ceremonial rituals that were so much a part of it all, fed and encouraged the natural creative urges of the Native people.

Many events could be the excuse for the giving of a potlatch — the building of a new longhouse, the raising of a mortuary pole, the birth of a baby, the coming of age of a daughter or a nephew, a marriage, succession to a leading position in the village, or the taking of new and more honorable names. Sometimes a potlatch was given to celebrate several events at the same time. When the government banned potlatch in 1870 because of its impoverishing effects, the blow struck deep into the structure of Northwest Coast society.

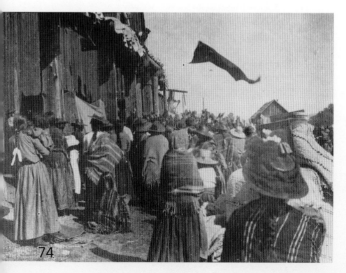

Quamichan potlatch, 1913. B.C. Provincial Museum.
Unlike other Northwest Coast cultures, the Coast Salish ended the formal gift giving aspect of the potlatch with an event called a scramble. At the time, a quantity of blankets and other goods were thrown to the guests in a playful free-for-all.

74

LIFE AND DEATH

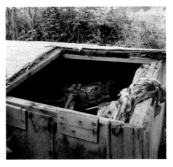

Coast Salish gravesite. The deceased was placed into a new cedar chest then carried to a designated site away from the main village. The box was elevated above the ground and commemorative carvings were left to mark the grave. The relatives of the deceased were careful to avoid activities that they believed could lead the soul back to them, as there was always a chance that the homesick spirit might try to take someone away with him.

Before the advent of the colonists and the days of the Indian reservations, when the Native people were frequently forced to abandon their villages and move to land set aside for them by the Government, life's pace was a slow and leisurely affair, with time being measured in moons and seasons, rather than in the minutes, hours, and days of the calendar month.

Most of the village sites were established on low benches, just above the high-water level of the sea, or above the flood level of the rivers. With the help of early photographs we can picture the long houses, with their lean-to roofs and plank sides, the large array of canoes pulled up on the beaches, sometimes turned over and covered with rush mats to protect them from the sun, and the great piles

Chatlip's Reserve burial site. Saanich Peninsula. Canadian Museum of Nature

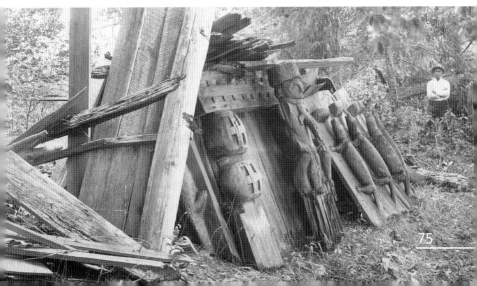

of empty clam shells, plus a certain amount of miscellaneous rubbish, including kelp-ends and other refuse.

Inside a longhouse we might have seen a woman using the northwestern spindle in order to produce a two-ply yarn. Another woman might have been at her loom busily weaving a blanket, with her baby nearby, snugly suspended in his cradle. On the floor, near one of the smoldering lodge fires, was an assortment of wooden cooking boxes and woven baskets along with a number of smooth round stones collected as just the right size and shape for use in heating water for cooking. Perhaps there would have been several men with no immediate outside duties might have been lolling near the fires, and children at play running in and out of the longhouse.

At different seasons the villages fairly hummed with activity, such as when the salmon were running. Fish had to be caught, dried and stored. Oil had to be extracted from the eulachon and salmon heads rendered down. Also, in season, there were clams to be dug and cooked, roots and bulbs to be found, and berries to be gathered.

But during the winter months there were periods of extended leisure and it was during these cold weather months that most of the games, dances, and other ceremonies and festivities took place.

When someone died they were considered to be among the "people who have gone to the dead". Prior to the coming of the settlers, the Coast Salish funeral involved a complicated ritual. The face of the deceased was painted red and black. His body, usually in a crouching position with the hands around the knees, was placed in a box that was raised about five feet from the ground. The box was then placed in a high tree, in canoes on isolated islands, or along parts of the shore where permanent cemeteries were established.

When the colonists came and the new authority under the Christian church was established, the ancient Indian burial practices ceased and the bodies were interred beneath the ground.

Coast Salish burial site.

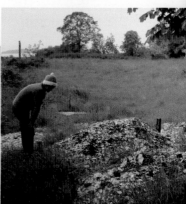

THE DORMANT PERIOD

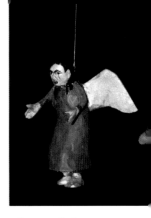

Coast Salish carving of an angel.

The Coast Salish, living as they did around the beaches and the waterways of some of the most desirable land in British Columbia and Washington State, were among the first of the Northwest Coast Indians to have their lives disrupted by the infiltration of non-Indians into their territory. That infiltration soon became a veritable tide, beginning with the Gold Rush days of the 1850s.

When settlements such as Victoria, New Westminster, Vancouver, and Seattle grew and expanded into Coast Salish territory, the Native inhabitants were moved from their ancestral villages onto government supervised reservation land. Only the Indians themselves could really understand the heartbreak of those early days when they were forced to accept a new religion and fit themselves into a lifestyle that was totally foreign and distasteful to them.

The Indians soon found they could no longer roam the land at will, hunting and fishing in what had formerly been their own territorial regions. Some of the best berry-picking and root-gathering

Gathering for a Sunday band concert. B.C. Provincial Museum.

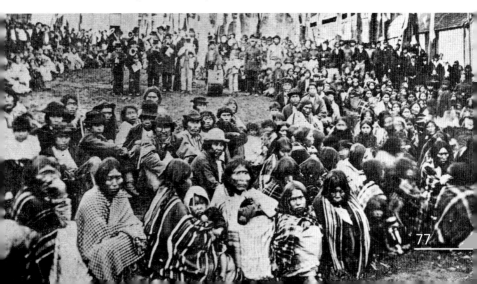

areas had suddenly become private property, owned by others. When the government banned the potlatch and took away the authorities of the chiefs and nobles of the villages, and the missionaries halted the practice of shamanism, the final blow had been delivered; Indian cultures collapsed in a state of chaotic disintegration.

The Coast Salish lived under a rigid caste system and according to early writers there were four classes evident in Coast Salish society — the princely class, the nobles, the commoners, and the slaves. The disintegration of their caste system effectively severed the Coast Salish connection to their cultural traditions. Once proud chiefs and nobles, shorn of most of their former prestige and authority, wandered about on the new reservations "like fallen eagles", according to one missionary observer.

There was no actual war between Indian and foreigners in British Columbia, although British gunboats went up and down the coast, firing on Indian villages when Governor Sir James Douglas faced some dissidence and found it necessary to cement and implement the new authority.

Further south, among the Coast Salish in Washington State, an actual war erupted, and the Puyaliup and Nisqually bands, backed up by the Duwamish and Klikitat, attacked the town of Seattle, then a mere collection of wooden buildings. The Puyaliup and Nisqually had good reason for the attack. Their land had been right in the middle of the colonists' settlements. Instead of being allowed to learn to farm there, with the help of tools and education, they were moved to a gravel bluff, with no water, no fertile land, and no pasture. When the Nisqually could not farm they found themselves literally starving; and the situation among the Puyaliup was little better.

Historians say the Indians might have taken Seattle if there had not been a warship in the harbor. Yet it was never the traditional policy of Northwest Coast Indians to occupy land other than their own. A sudden attack, a few killings, the taking of slaves, and a quick retreat with as little loss as possible was the only type of war waged in Indian days.

In the attack on Seattle, the Indians burned two houses, shot two men and drove off the cattle. This small war took place in the winter of 1855-56 and the attack on Seattle, which the Indians at first regarded as a victory that might hopefully scare the foreigners away, resulted in a wholesale disaster for them.

Leschi, the leader of the Nisqually, had led 200 Indians against 600 fighters on the settlers' side, including the troopers. The Indians, with no home base, were camped in the swamps at the base of the Cascade Mountains. They died like flies from starvation and finally Leschi led the gaunt men and women and dying children up over the mountain ice and back into the coastal plain. There they surrendered, Leschi was hanged, and the last embers of Indian resistance died away.

The years 1850 to 1860 marked the beginnings of a long cultural sleep for the Coast Salish. Some left their reservations and camped as near as they could get to their old villages, eking out a living by fishing, gathering clams, roots and berries, and selling whatever they could to settlers. They even traded their beautifully woven baskets, now mere curios in the new order of things, in exchange for cast off clothing and a little money.

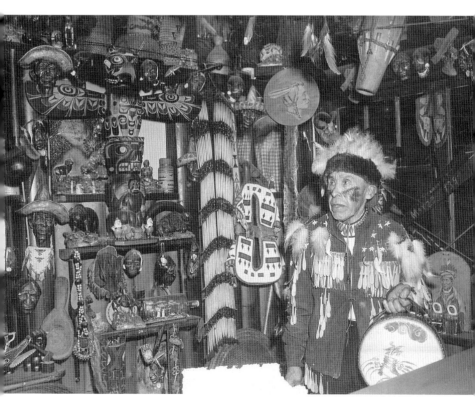

Chief Dominic Charlie. (Photo: Reg Ashwell)

REBIRTH OF ART AND CULTURE

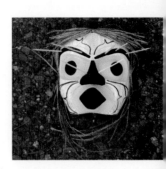

*Bumble Bee mask by
Judy Hill*

The 1920s were probably the lowest years in the cultural history of the Northwest Indians. By 1930 the Coast Salish had almost abandoned their traditional ceremonial costumes in favor of those of the Prairie Indians, who remain the stereotype of the non-Indian's image of the noble Aboriginal of long ago.

Robes of otter, bearskin, lynx, or marten, blankets of creamy wool, and glistening capes of duck or loon feathers gave way to fringed and beaded buckskins; and the legendary Coast Salish hats, conical in shape and made of human hair adorned at the crown with two duck or loon feathers, were replaced with a colorful but non-traditional headdress of eagle feathers, or whatever feathers were available.

Venerable chiefs and nobles such as Chief August Jack Khatsahlano, who was the last of forty great shamans of the ancient

*Chief Dominic Charlie wearing Plains
Indian headdress.* (Photo: Jilek)

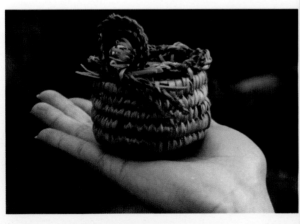

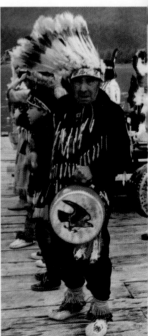

*Contemporary basket woven by
Angela Marston.*

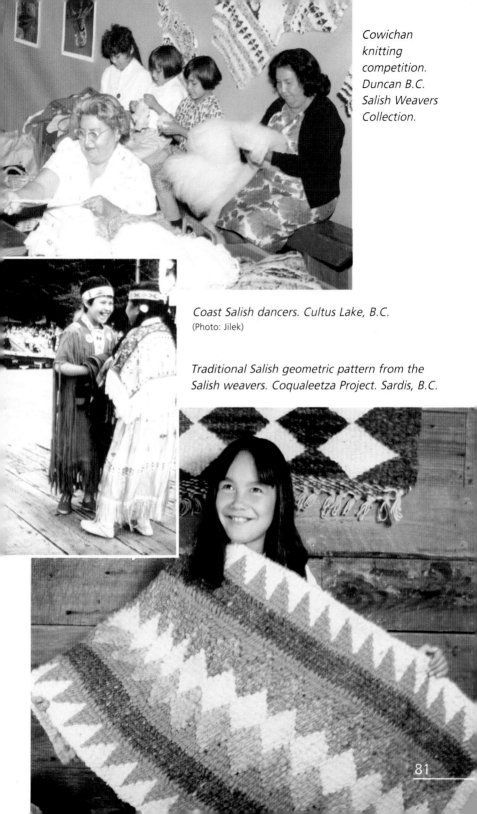

Cowichan knitting competition. Duncan B.C. Salish Weavers Collection.

Coast Salish dancers. Cultus Lake, B.C.
(Photo: Jilek)

Traditional Salish geometric pattern from the Salish weavers. Coqualeetza Project. Sardis, B.C.

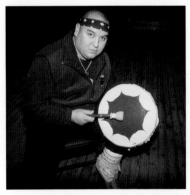

Drummer performing at the Xa:ytem Native Heritage Centre.

Order of Dancers of the Squamish Indians, and Chief Mary Capilano of the Squamish band, whose Indian name was Lay-hu-lette (which means "the beginning of the world"), continued to cling to the old beliefs and customs, and to exert a powerful influence among their people. Chief Mathias Joe and Dominic Charlie, the renowned interpreter of Coast Salish dances, were also instrumental in helping to maintain a link with the colorful past.

With the collapse of Indian cultures under the foreign influence, Coast Salish art, like that of all the Northwest Coast tribes, languished for many years until it almost reached the point of extinction. However, gradually over the years, the attitude of non-Indian people toward their Indian brothers underwent a profound change and a new interest was kindled in Indian art.

This change probably began with the recognition, in the late 1920s, of the work of artist Emily Carr. Miss Carr had traveled extensively for many years among the Native people of British Columbia, painting Indian villages and totem poles. The wild beauty and power of Northwest Coast Native carvings was dramatically captured and faithfully portrayed in the hundreds of water colors and oils this courageous and talented woman left as a legacy to all Canadians.

Coast Salish artists began carving small "tourist totems" for sale in gift shops, but the art had little focus or meaning at that point. However, as artists began to connect to their heritage and develop

(below) Opportunities for learning about Coast Salish culture are provided by museum school programs and cultural centers such as the Xa:ytem Native Heritage Centre.

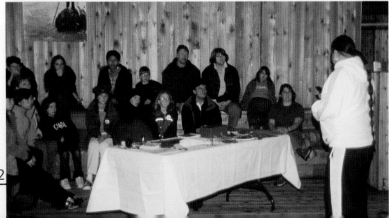

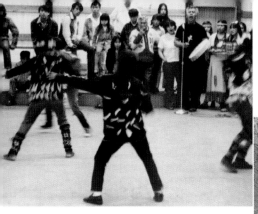

(left) Young people carry on the traditions of the elders.

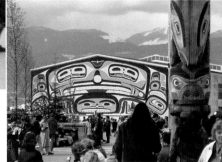

(right) "Habitat". Vancouver B.C.

(below) North Vancouver Powwow. These well-attended events celebrate the past, while creating new traditions that will be carried on into the future.

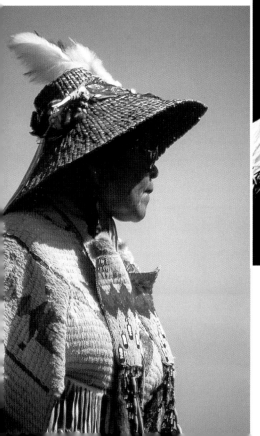

(above) North Vancouver powwow dancer from the Squamish band.

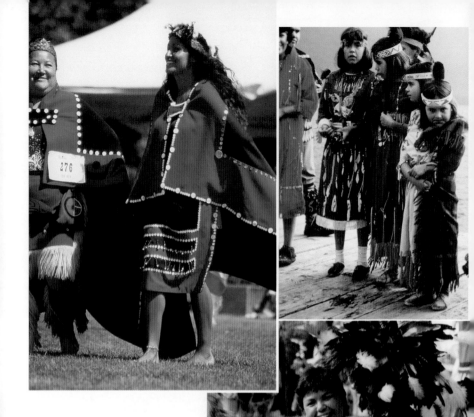

Contemporary Coast Salish powwows.

their skills, interest in Coast Salish art finally gathered momentum and it is now enjoying a well-deserved renaissance.

The art of the Coast Salish has been described as a direct art, and carvers of past eras displayed little in common with the decorative, two-dimensional art of the northern coastal tribes. House posts, grave figures, and ceremonial dance masks were usually plainly carved and simply designed with a sparing use of paint, yet much of the work revealed a stark beauty and emanated a power which lifted it to comparable levels with the best in Northwest Coast art.

Many of the old Coast Salish masks, notably the legendary skhwaykhwey mask — a much-revered mask used in the secret society dances — compared favorably with the sophisticated northern style masks of other Northwest Coast tribes. Deeply carved, and richly designed and painted, their owners jealously guard these masks, and the history of the skhwaykhwey mask is deeply rooted in Coast Salish art and culture. Today they are rarely made and continue to be much coveted by collectors of West Coast Native art.

With their once-decimated populations on the upswing and the potlatch again legalized in 1951 by an enlightened federal government, new incentives to re-establish Coast Salish art and culture have grown rapidly. Much credit must be given to Master Carver and Elder Simon Charlie, of the Cowichan Indian band, for his dedication to the preservation of the traditions, art, and culture of his people.

Simon was born at Koksilah, a few miles south of Duncan on Vancouver Island, on November 15, 1919, and passed away in Duncan on May 3, 2005. His vigorously direct and powerfully carved totem poles, portraying the Cowichan legends Thunderbird, Spirit Dancer, Bear, Killer Whale, and Frog can be found in the Parliament Buildings in Ottawa, and from Washington State to New York, Chicago, throughout Europe, South America, Japan, New Zealand, and Australia. One of his greatest works, a Cowichan Indian welcoming figure, stands inside the main doors of the Royal BC Museum in Victoria, welcoming visitors to the museum. In times past, such a figure, which is that of a man with his arms raised in a welcoming salute, might stand on a beach to welcome guests attending a potlatch.

Modern day Coast Salish art is changing and has moved closer to the stylized designs of the north, and there are now many modern day Coast Salish artists whose work is contributing significantly in furthering Coast Salish cultural aspirations.

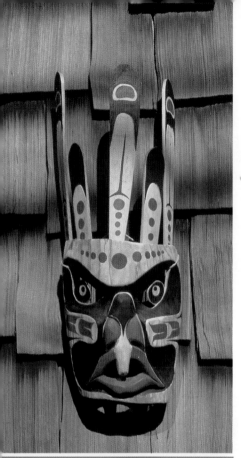

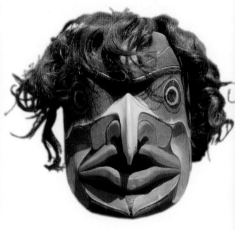

Masks by Coast Salish artist Simon Charlie.

These pages are presented to honor the lifelong commitment to art, culture and humanity by legendary Coast Salish carver Simon Charlie who passed away in 2005.

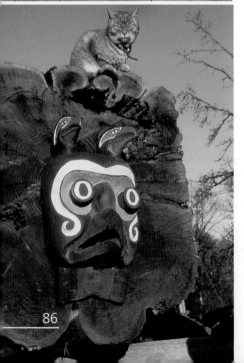

(left) One of Simon Charlie's prized Skhway-Khwey masks used in secret societies' ceremonies.

The characteristics of a dancer's spirit helper would be expressed by the face paint and headdress that the dancer wore. Masks could be purchased or gained through inheritance and sometimes an individual would carve a mask representing his own spirit helper. Although these masks could be passed on, the associated helping spirit could not. It remains with the original owner.

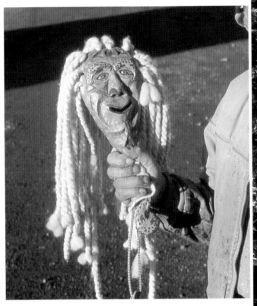

Simon Charlie holding a salmon rattle.

(right) Totem of thunderbird, whale and bear by Simon Charlie. Duncan, B.C.

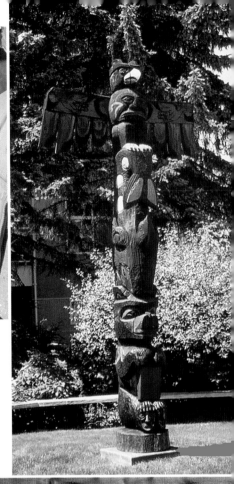

Thunderbird totem by Simon Charlie.

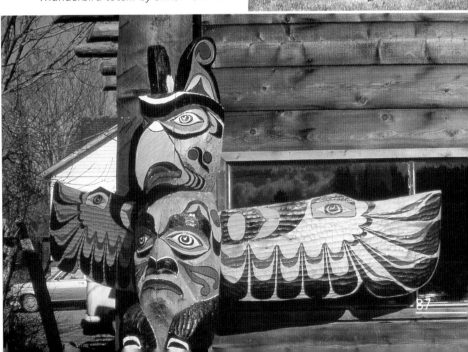

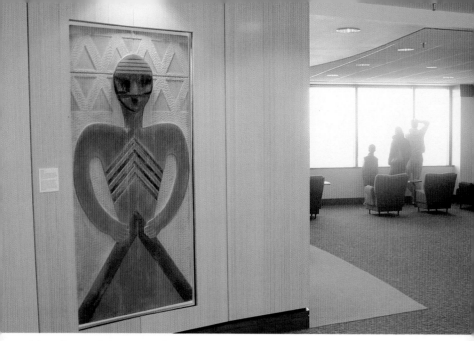

(above) **Transition I** (1988)
Marvin Oliver. Carved cedar panel.
72 ¾ x 37 ½ x 2 inches. City of Seattle,
Portable Works Collection.
(Photo: Marvin Oliver)

(below) **Transition II** (1988)
Marvin Oliver. Cast glass panel.
72 x 34 ¼ x 2 inches. City of Seattle,
Portable Works Collection.
(Photo: Marvin Oliver)

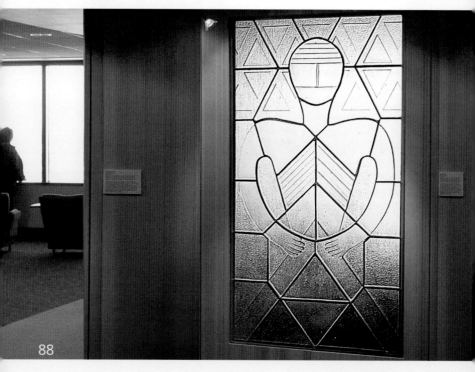

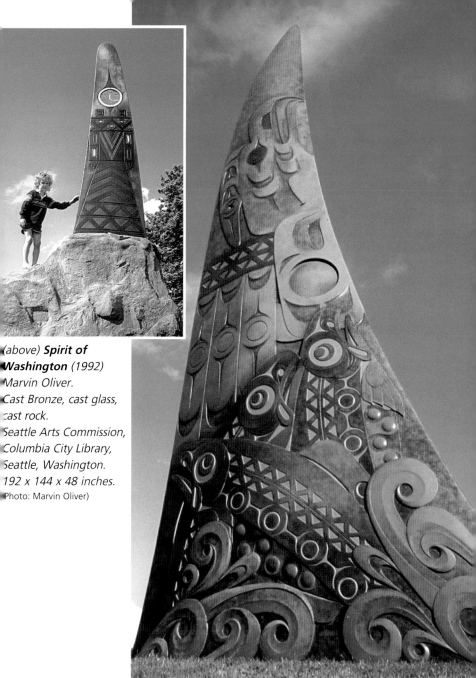

(above) **Spirit of Washington** *(1992)*
Marvin Oliver.
Cast Bronze, cast glass, cast rock.
Seattle Arts Commission, Columbia City Library, Seattle, Washington.
192 x 144 x 48 inches.
(Photo: Marvin Oliver)

Spirit of Our Youth *(1996)*
Marvin Oliver. Cast bronze and earthworks,
312 x 96 x 24 inches. King County Arts Commission,
Seattle, Washington.
(Photo: Marvin Oliver)

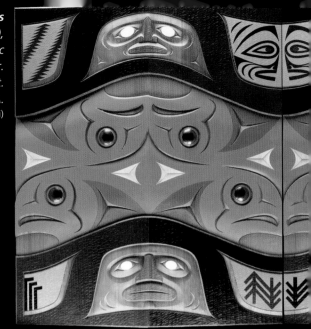

(right) **Northwind's Fishing Weir** *(2005), Carved red cedar, acrylic paint, copper and antler. 44 x 144 feet. Seattle, WA, USA.*
(Photo: Kenji Nagai)

(below) **Spawning Salmon** *(1990), Original design, cast and commissioned for the Sechelt Indian Band by The Dominion Company, Sechelt, BC.*
(Photo: Bob Mathieson)

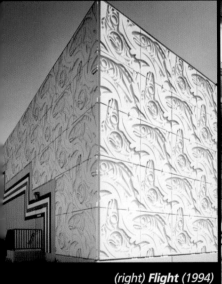

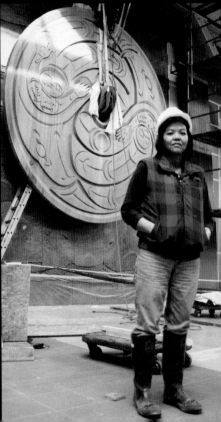

(right) **Flight** *(1994) Carved red cedar spindle whorl. 17' diameter. Commissioned by Vancouver International Airport Authority for the new International Terminal Building. Susan Point, artist, in foreground.*
(Photo: Jeff Cannell)

90

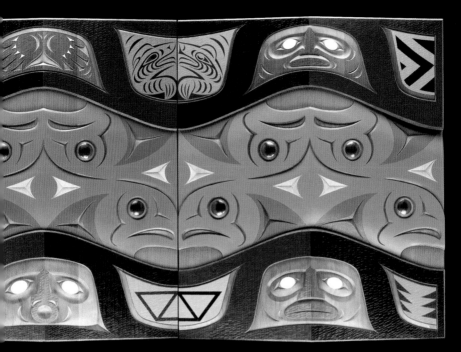

"Salish art has re-emerged over the last decade and is now recognized as a prominent art form of the Pacific Northwest; I believe that it will continue to flourish because so many Salish artists are rediscovering their roots and the rich legacy left by our ancestors.

Salish artisans are now respecting the traditional Salish design elements that define our unique style among the other Northwest Coast Native art forms. A contemporary movement is evolving based on our past ensuring a proud Salish mark for countless generations to come. As a Salish artist, I feel proud and fortunate to have contributed to the artistic journey of my people."

— Susan Point

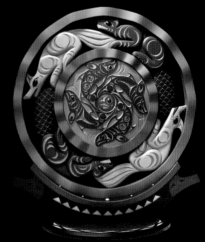

(above) **The Beaver and the Mink** (2004), Two sided sculpture, carved red cedar, paint and patinated copper, 7.5 feet high. Commissioned by the Government of Canada as a gift to the Smithsonian Institute in Washington DC, to celebrate the opening of the new National Museum of the American Indian

(Photo: Kenji Nagai)

91

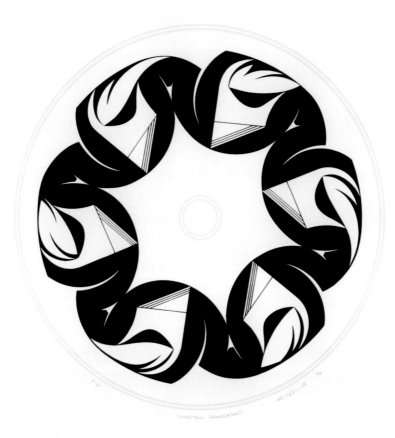

Connecting Generations (2004)
Serigraph (Edition of 65) 16 x 16 inches
Kelly Cannell

Kelly Cannell is a Coast Salish artist who from birth has been exposed to the endeavors and teachings of her mother Susan A. Point. Kelly is becoming fluent with the use of Coast Salish traditional elements. In 1999 Kelly was commissioned by Canadian Airlines to create an original logo for their team t-shirts in the annual World Airline Road Race. In recent years Kelly has created several collaborative screen prints with Susan and has worked on a number of her own private commissions. In 2004 she was selected as one of the successful entrants (along with Susan) in a competition to design new storm sewer covers for the City of Vancouver.

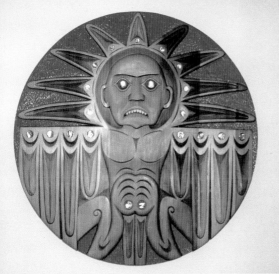

Salish spindle whorl, by artist Luke Marston. It is titled "Man Who Fell From The Sky" and is carved of red cedar, inset with abalone.

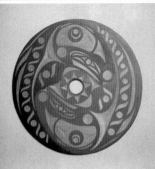 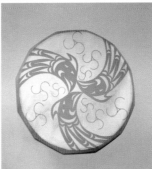

Two spindle whorls. The one on the right features Thunderbird, while the left one has Raven. Campbell River Gift Shop. The figures represented on spindle whorls are often carvings of Spirit Helpers.

(right) Double Thunderbird spindle whorl located at Stonington Gallery, Seattle, WA. It is inset with abalone and carved in red cedar. Artist: John Marston.

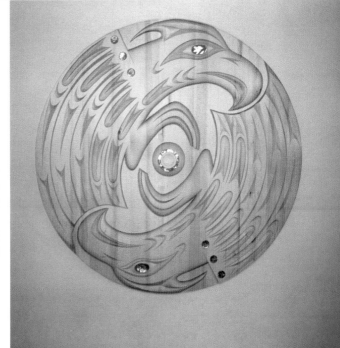

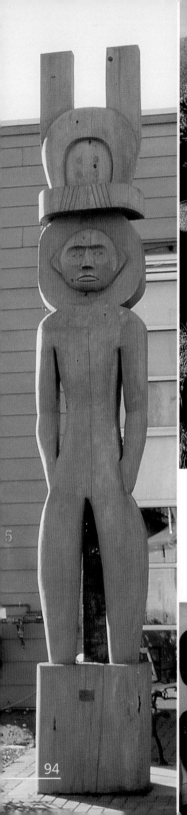

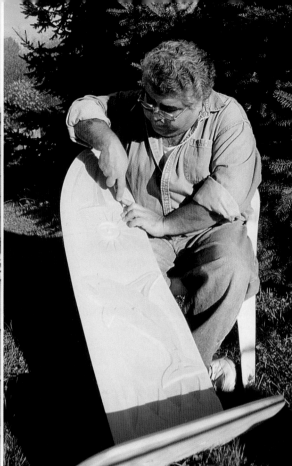

Artists such as Herb Cook are reviving the culture by carving traditional Coast Salish forms.

Luke Marston of Vancouver Island at work on a storage box.

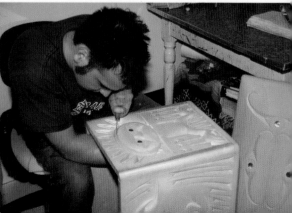

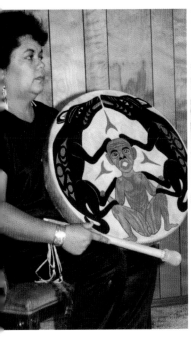

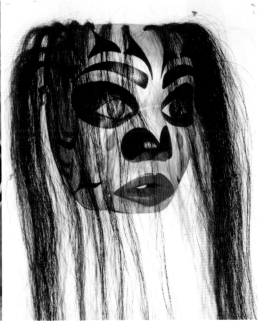

Shaman drum, with shaman and two wolf spirit helpers, created by Jane Marston.

Coast Salish design. Horsehair and alder mask entitled, "Cry Baby of the Sea". Jane Marston.

Salmon-head mask carved by artist, John Marston.

Cedar bark plaited hat by Angela Marston.

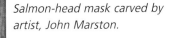

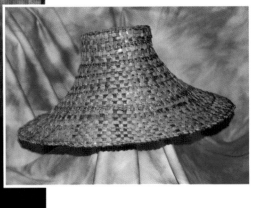

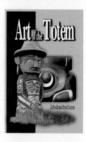
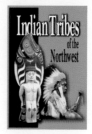
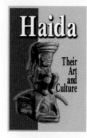
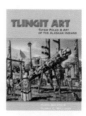
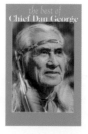
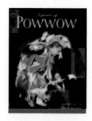
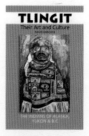
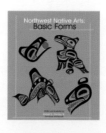
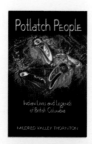